BOOKS BY MARK STRAND

POETRY

Blizzard of One   1998

Dark Harbor   1993

*Reasons for Moving, Darker, &
The Sargentville Notebook*   1992

The Continuous Life   1990

Selected Poems   1980

The Late Hour   1978

The Story of Our Lives   1973

Darker   1970

Reasons for Moving   1968

Sleeping with One Eye Open
1964

PROSE

The Weather of Words   2000

Mr. and Mrs. Baby   1985

The Monument   1978

TRANSLATIONS

Travelling in the Family
(with Thomas Colchie)   1986
(Poems by Carlos Drummond de
Andrade)

The Owl's Insomnia   1973
(Poems by Rafael Alberti)

ART BOOKS

Edward Hopper   1993

William Bailey   1987

Art of the Real   1983

FOR CHILDREN

Rembrandt Takes a Walk   1986

The Night Book   1985

The Planet of Lost Things   1982

ANTHOLOGIES

The Golden Ecco Anthology
1994

The Best American Poetry 1991
(with David Lehman)

Another Republic
(with Charles Simic)   1976

New Poetry of Mexico
(with Octavio Paz)   1970

*The Contemporary American
Poets*   1969

The Weather of Words

The Weather of Words

POETIC INVENTION

by

Mark Strand

Alfred A. Knopf
New York   2001

This Is a Borzoi Book
Published by Alfred A. Knopf

Copyright © 2000 by Mark Strand

*All rights reserved under International and Pan-American
Copyright Conventions. Published in the United States by Alfred A.
Knopf, a division of Random House, Inc., New York, and simultaneously
in Canada by Random House of Canada Limited, Toronto.
Distributed by Random House, Inc., New York.*

www.randomhouse.com

*Knopf, Borzoi Books, and the colophon are registered trademarks
of Random House, Inc.*

*Owing to limitations of space, all permissions to reprint previously
published material may be found on pages 147–8.*

*Library of Congress
Cataloging-in-Publication Data*
Strand, Mark.
*The weather of words : poetic invention /
by Mark Strand.*
p. cm.
ISBN 0-375-70970-3
1. Poetics. 2. Imagination. 3. Poetry. I. Title.
PN1042.S767 2000
809.1—dc21 99-35815
CIP

*Manufactured in the United States of America
Published February 8, 2000
First Paperback Edition, November 23, 2001*

The author wishes to thank Joanna Klink, without whose help this book would not exist. Her
editorial guidance was invaluable.

M.S.

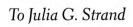

To Julia G. Strand

Contents

CONTENTS

The Weather of Words

A Poet's Alphabet

A is for absence. It is sometimes—but not always—nice to think that other people may be talking about you when you are not present, that you are the subject of a conversation you have not steered in your direction and whose evolution depends on your absence. This is what happens to the famous. And to the dead. They can be the life of the party and never show up. For those neither famous nor dead, at the bottom of their yearning to be absent is the hope that they will be missed. Being missed suggests being loved. True, not to be the active or living recipient of what one craves may seem a sorry fate. But it takes no effort. Hang around and you interfere with the love that could be yours; die and you clear a space for yourself.

B is for before, the acknowledged antecedent of now, the innocent shape of earlier, the vague and beautiful cousin of "when," the tragic mother of "will become," the suicide of "too late."

. . .

C is for Canada, the country of my birth, of my earliest memories, where my parents lived out their last years, where they are buried. It was the backdrop to their sorrow and was so big, so empty, that every day they lived there, they could count on being lost.

D is for Dante, who has not influenced me, which is too bad. On the other hand, I am not sure what the influence of Dante might be, and I would think it quite strange to read somewhere that one of my contemporaries had been influenced by him. How very grand, I would think. But death, being so much more approachable—either here or just around the bend—has always been an influence. What I mean to say is that death is common. If you are having a good time and you conceive the possibility that the good time will end, then you are concerned with death, though in a mild and unremarkable way. But what I want to get to is something else: that death is the central concern of lyric poetry. Lyric poetry reminds us that we live in time. It tells us that we are mortal. It celebrates or recognizes moods, ideas, events only as they exist in passing. For what meaning would anything have outside of time? Even when poetry celebrates something joyful, it bears the news that the particular joy is over. It is a long memorial, a valedictory to each discrete moment on earth. But its power is at variance with what it celebrates. For it is not just that we mourn the passage of time but that we are somehow isolated from the weight of time, and when we read poems, during those brief moments of absorption, the thought of death seems pain-less, even beautiful.

E is for endings, endings to poems, last words designed to release us back into our world with the momentary illusion that no harm has been done. They are various, and inscribe themselves in the ghostly aftermath of any work of art. Much of what we love about poems, regardless of their sub-ject, is that they leave us with a sense of renewal, of more life. Life, on the other hand, prepares us for nothing, and leaves us nowhere to go. It stops.

F is for fashion, literary fashion, which marks the writing of a period or an age, and which is virtually inescapable, as inescapable as its sister Death. Even originality will be only what a period accepts as original, which means that it has been anticipated to a certain extent by what it desires to sep-arate itself from. There is no way around it. And if we believe we are oblivious to a contemporary style, we are only more likely to embody its standards. And if we think to dis-tance ourselves from current fashion by finding another fashion from which to fashion ourselves, chances are it will be the one that current fashion predicted we'd pick.

. . .

G is for a garden, but which garden I don't know. Maybe the corner of a particular garden; maybe a garden in which there is a chair that waits for someone to sit. It is not an ideal garden, not a garden of Eden, nor a hellish garden like Bomarzo, nor ordered like the Doria Pamphily in Rome, nor disheveled like the Boboli gardens in Florence. It is not a backyard. It must be what I think when I say "garden" to myself: a green space that is contained and that will contain some of the poem's action, or none of it. Maybe there are trees, maybe the leaves have fallen. There could be snow, and some juncos may have gathered around the base of the mountain ash, which grows there. I don't know. It will be a while before I do.

H is for Hades, which I like to think of as an influence because of all places it strikes me as the most poetic. A last resort, a high-walled kingdom, it has one major disadvantage—the weather, which is windy, dark, and cold. Its major advantage is the great amount of leisure time it offers. It is straight down, under the world, and is the immortal resting place of souls. More important: it is where the dead wait for a new life, a second chance, where they wait to be remembered, reborn in the minds of the living. It is a hopeful place. And *Thanatos*, or what we think of as the Greek personification of death, is not really a personification, but a mist or veil or cloud that separates the still living person from life. For the Greeks, who had no word for irreversible death, one did not die; one darkened.

I is for immortality, which for some poets is a necessary and believable form of compensation. Presumably miserable in this life, they will be remembered when the rest of us are long forgotten. None of them asks about the quality of that remembrance—what it will be like to crouch in the dim hallways of somebody's mind until the moment of recollection occurs, or to be lifted off suddenly and forever into the pastures of obscurity. Most poets know better than to concern themselves with such things. They know the chances are better than good that their poems will die when they do and never be heard of again, that they'll be replaced by poems sporting a new look in a language more current. They also know that even if individual poems die, though in some cases slowly, poetry will continue: that its subjects, its constant themes, are less liable to change than fashions in language, and that this is where an alternate, less lustrous immortality might be. We all know that a poem can influence other poems, remain alive in them, just as previous poems are alive in it. Could we not say, therefore, that individual poems succeed most by encouraging revisions of themselves and inducing their own erasure? Yes, but is this immortality, or simply a purposeful way of being dead?

J is for the joy of writing. As if there were such a thing! The truth is that writing is joyless, at least for me, for when I think of my happiest moments, not one occurred while I was writing. J is for jasmine, for the sweet torment of being overcome by its scent. I remember how it was when I was young:

when twilight would give way to darkness, I would lose myself among the jasmine's yellow stars. And I would drift in a sensuous version of the galaxy, always further and further away. That was joy, that drifting away.

K is for Kafka, and the authority of his peculiar realism. In the first paragraph of "The Metamorphosis," the inexplicable has happened. Gregor Samsa wakens to find himself transformed into a gigantic insect. Our astonishment is immediately tempered by the narrator's calm as he describes the "new" Gregor, for he is much more interested in having us visualize Gregor than in having us feel anything towards him. Over the course of the story, as Gregor disintegrates, our feelings for him increase—somewhat. But in the beginning we know only that Gregor has undergone a bizarre transformation. It is not just that he felt like an insect or that his waking was an illusion and he was still asleep in one of his uneasy dreams. He was in fact an insect. The story's power depends on our acceptance of this singular truth. If Gregor screamed on first seeing his new body, we would immediately cease to believe in him. It would indicate that he knew or felt the extent of his misfortune, when actually his misfortune had only just begun. Kafka's methodical, dispassionate description of Gregor, which sets the tone as well as the terms of the story, makes it very hard for the reader to reverse—even if he should want to—the story's outrageous premise. It would be too much work. The facts insist that whatever doubts we have about what happened are bound to be groundless. We are safer, for the moment, if we believe in Gregor's misfortune than if we did not—for if we did not, what would we believe in? There would be no story, and what is almost as bad—no universe that accommodates the unexpected.

L is for lake. I prefer the ocean and some of the rivers I've seen, but for writing I like the manageable water of lakes. A lake is a more flexible prop. It doesn't demand the respect of the ocean, which compels us to fairly predictable responses; that is, we too easily slip into feelings of awe or peace or whatever. Nor does it tease us with hints of the infinite. A lake can be made to fit what the poem's topography demands. Rivers will generally run through a poem, or carry it along, and they tend to resist formal containment, which is why they are so frequently (but mistakenly) likened to life. They also tend to be shallow, a feature which might be equated with life as well, but not with poetry. So, for a body of water, give me a lake, a great lake or even a salt lake, where water can be still, where reflection is possible, where one can kneel at the edge, look down, and see oneself. It is an old story.

M is for music, which I listen to through earphones when I write prose, but not when I write poetry. What I listen to again and again are the slurred confections of Delius, Wagner, or Tchaikovsky. Their music is nothing that jeopardizes my need or my ability to concentrate. Yet I am stirred by it, seduced into a vague rhythmic certainty. Everything is better; everything rises to an occasion that exceeds even the jammy excess of the music. I write as if on an endless sea of surges and satisfactions.

N is for Neruda, who was a genius but in whose writing beauty and banality are inextricably mixed. His poems are a sort of wishful thinking. To read him is to participate in the verbal correction of what are universally perceived as social or natural inequities. Mundane items, modified by adjectives denoting the rare or celestial, are elevated to a realm of exceptional value. A toad is melancholy, wine is intelligent, a lemon is like a cathedral. He is a cosmetician of the ordinary. When we read him, we are happy because everything has attained to a condition of privilege. The universe is good after all. Neruda's verbal utopia, depending on one's gullibility, is a harmless antidote to a harrowing century. His genial reductions have moved people to simple and accommodating attitudes towards poetry who otherwise would have no use for it. N is also for nothing, which, in its all-embracing modesty, is the manageable sister of everything. Ah, nothing! About which anything can be said, and is. An absence that knows no bounds. The climax of inaction. It has been perhaps the central influence on my writing. It is the original of sleep and the end of life.

O is for Oblivion. I feel as strongly about it as I do about nothing. Forgetfulness, the fullness of forgetting, the possibilities of forgottenness. The freedom of unmindfulness. It is the true beginning of poetry. It is the blank for which the will wills. And O, lest I forget, O is also for Ovid, *Il Naso*, the first of the great exiles, whose book of changes, whose elevation of changing to a central place in the kingdom of the imagination, has made me wish to mention him, even if he has not directly influenced the poems I write. After all, what could I take from his beautiful telling of Echo and Narcissus or Jason and Medea? How could I duplicate the Song of Polyphemus? Maybe if I worked very hard I could produce a stumbling version of his fluency, and maybe a pale likeness of a few of his monstrous particulars, but never the two together. He was an effortless surrealist, a poet of boundless charm. And all it got him from the puritanical Augustus was exile to the shores of the Black Sea, in a place called Tomis.

P is for the passage of time. It is also for the secret passage that leads out of time into the stillness of what has not yet been named into being, the passage that leads to the birthplace of poems. It is for the passage that is the route of my passing, my having been, and for the passage of places into history, and through history into forgottenness.

. . .

Q is for the questionable in matters relating to poetry, lines or images for which no precedent comes immediately to mind and whose virtues seem equally elusive. In time, our wayward lines and images may become our greatest successes, the true signs of our authorship. But when we are young we are slow to trust ourselves, preferring to sound like more established writers. For that is how we make sure that what we have written is indeed poetry. Eventually, we learn to mistrust what is patently derived, and we cultivate what we first perceived as weakness. It is the oddity of our poems, their idiosyncrasy, their lapses into a necessary awkwardness, their ultimate frailty, that charms and satisfies.

R is for Rilke, whose poems I read for inspiration of a peculiar sort, since what I get mainly when I read him is a sense of uplift, some lavish and ornate attempt to locate being, certain moments of ecstatic insight close to the truth, or what I believe to be true. I feel the unutterable has found a place in what has been uttered. I am thinking of Part I of *The Spanish Trilogy*, and the ninth of *The Duino Elegies*, and "Orpheus. Eurydice. Hermes," and "Lament," and "Evening."

S is for something that supplies a vacancy, which I might fill. It has a verbal presence that my own immediate appetite or ambition subverts, misreads, or makes into an appealing void, a space only I can elaborate on. I begin with something as if it were nothing (or nothing as if it were something) because, often, what I have chosen as my starting point makes no sense to others, as when, say, I open up my Wallace Stevens and my eye alights upon "shaken sleep" or "pearled" or "later reason." S is also for Stevens. I have always turned to his poems, reading parts of them, skipping on to others, finding them congenial despite my fickleness, my impatience. I admire Stevens and Frost equally among American poets, but I read them differently. Stevens influences me, but I do not think that Frost does. Frost's diction is given over to voice, a continuous sound that tempers verbal color. In a Frost poem, it is its spokenness that counts, that overrides even those periodic passages of vatic emphasis. Words are submerged into clusters of sense, so that some tonal character can assert itself—an argument, an extended gesture that relies on the order and direction of what is said. In Stevens, argument tends to be discontinuous, hidden, mysterious, or simply not there. More often, what we experience is the power of the word or the phrase to enchant. The rhetorical design of his poems points to explanation or annunciation. But there is no urgency that constructs "nextness"—what comes next is a possibility, a choice, another invitation to imagine.

T is for tedium, and by tedium I do not mean the heartsickness of Leopardi's *noia*, or the deadening emptiness of Baudelaire's *ennui*. I do not mean those encounters with the void that leave the sufferer in despair or, as we are more likely to say, in a deep depression. By tedium I mean no more than the household variety of boredom, the sweet monotony of daily life. My tedium is a luxury. In its arms, I am passive. I sit around and peruse a book, or check the fridge, or do a puzzle. Pretty soon my laziness palls. I try to extricate myself. I drink some coffee. This gets me working. And I say to myself that it couldn't be done without tedium, most benign of pressures.

U is for Utah, the western surround of my indispensable tedium and, in many ways, its inspiration. Utah is everything that my life before moving there was not. It is slow, which gives my tedium its requisite lack of energy. Charles Wright says somewhere, "There's so little to say, and so much time in which to say it." Well, Utah gives one that feeling in the dryness and harshness of its terrain, in the largeness of its sky, in its yellow-and-redness.

V is for Vergil, who took what was a fleeting bit of background music in Homer, that strain of elegy, and made it the central, inescapable condition of the *Aeneid*. All those exquisite passages of lament and exhaustion, of time passing and life lost, all that elegiac grace that seems to make of the *Aeneid* a long lyric, mark Vergil as the first great gardener in the landscape of grief, and the father of pastoral elegy. Is it a negligible irony or not that our vision of pastoral elegy derives so much from the beauty of the Underworld? I know only that any description of landscape has within it an elusiveness, an unobtainableness that goes beyond the seasonal cycles and what they mean, and that suggests something like the constant flourishing of a finality in which we are confronted with the limits of our feeling. We end up lamenting the loss of something we never possessed.

W is for what might have been or what I might have written. Can I be influenced by what I might have done but didn't?—as if the choice to write what I couldn't or didn't were still before me. It is not as if what I might have written exists, even as a possibility. Still, I sometimes say to myself that if I hadn't done this, I might have done that, even if I don't know what that might be. What I might have written stands in shadowy, sober judgment of what I have written. It gathers whatever self it has and comes, unbidden, to visit me. W is also for what I would never have written because I could not have, even in a thousand years. A conceivable source of unhappiness, it is in fact a relief. Think if I had written the first hundred or so lines in Book XIII of the 1805 *Prelude*, what a great poet I would be. I would have to destroy everything else I had written to keep people from saying, "What a falling off there has been in Strand's work." So I wouldn't be me, and I would not have my poems, and I would have nothing to worry about. W is for Wordsworth, who wrote what I didn't and couldn't and won't.

X is for crossing out, which is hardly an influence. It is, however, a sobering activity, one that I wish I did less of, but which my detractors probably feel I should do more of. But crossing out is not so bad. A canceled line looks a lot less precious than it did before the drastic measure was taken. One can grow to like getting rid of this or that. It is like dieting. On the other hand, lopping off an arm or leg is not a satisfactory way to lose weight.

Y is for why. Why is the question we ask ourselves again and again. Why are we here and not there? Why am I me? Why not a goldfish in a fish tank in a restaurant somewhere on the outskirts of Des Moines?

Z is for the zenith, the ultimate influence. It is the highest point in the sky directly overhead; it is what some hats point towards, yet what umbrellas deny; it is the eventual extreme of highest thoughts, and the divine refutation of earth and earthiness; it is the utmost point of contact with utmost otherness; it is the final resting place and celestial terminus of poems worth having.

Fantasia on the Relations Between Poetry and Photography

I / ON THE SADNESS OF A FAMILY PHOTOGRAPH

I have a photograph of my mother, my sister, and myself, taken when I was about four years old and when my mother was thirty-two or so. My sister and I are standing on what must be the front walk of our house then, in front of a hedge, and my mother is crouched in the middle with an arm around each of us. It must be spring, because I am wearing shorts and a long-sleeved shirt, which is buttoned, probably as a concession to neatness, at the neck. My sister, who was then about two and a half, is wearing a coat that stops just above her knees. The sleeves are too long. It must be noon or close to it: our common shadow is directly beneath us. My mother's hair is dark and she is smiling. The light spills over her forehead and rides the top of her cheeks; a patch of it rests on one side of her chin. The light falls the same way over my sister's face and mine. And all of our eyes are in shadow in precisely the same way. I have stared and stared at this photograph, and each time I have felt a deep and inexplicable rush of sadness. Is it that my mother, who holds us and whose hand I hold, is now dead? Or is it that she is so young, so happy, so proud of her children? Is it that the three of us are momentarily bound by the way the light distributes itself in identical ways over each of our faces, binding us together, proclaiming our unity for a moment in a past that was just ours and that no one now can share? Or is it simply that we look a bit out-of-date? Or that whatever we were at the moment catches the heart merely by being over? I suppose all are good reasons for feeling sad, and they may account in some part for my feelings, but there is something else that I am responding to. It is the presence of the photographer. It is for him that my mother allows herself to be so spontaneously present, to show an aspect of herself uncomplicated by any withholding, any sign of sorrow. And it is towards him that I lean, to him that I want to run. But who was he? He must have been my father, I keep saying to myself, my father who, in those days, seemed always absent, always on the road, selling one of the news services to the small-town papers in Pennsylvania. So, it is not that a moment of sweetness has passed that makes me sad. It is that the one most powerfully present is not in the picture, but exists conjecturally, as an absence. Something else that moves me about this photograph is the way it is so much about the moment in which it was taken. Like childhood itself, it is innocent of the future. I feel an enormous sympathy for the small boy I was, and I feel guilty that his likeness should be served up years later to his older self. I existed, at that moment, not for my gaze today but for the photographer at the moment of the photograph. In other words, I was not posing. I couldn't, because I could not anticipate a future for that moment; I lived, like most children, in a perpetual present. I could hold still, but I could not pose. And in my holding still, I manifest a tremendous eagerness to break free, to embrace my father who is nowhere in the picture.

II / ON THE SADNESS OF ANOTHER FAMILY PHOTO

I have another photograph of my mother, taken when she was twenty-four. She sits with her mother on the beach in Miami. Neither is in a bathing suit. My grandmother wears a sweater over a blouse and skirt, my mother a dark something-or-other. In the background, a lifeguard sits to the side of a white wooden lookout station with a canvas canopy on top. My mother stares directly into the lens, as if at that second obeying the photographer's request to look at the camera. Why is this such a sad photograph? My mother looks more beautiful than she ever has. And she is smiling. Even her mother, for whom I always heard happiness was unobtainable, seems happy. What then? It is another case of the missing person. And in this photograph, I am the one who is missing. I was not yet born, nor conceived, nor had my mother even met my father. That my mother was happily alive despite my absence does not come as any surprise, but on some level it does offer a rebuke to my presence and seems to question my own importance. After all, I knew her only in relation to myself, so there is a part of me that feels left out, even jealous. There is something else, too. I see her not as my mother but as a beautiful young woman, and I think how I wish I had known her then. For she might have liked me, and I might have liked her. We might even have been lovers. It is the impossibility of this erotic connection that is saddening. For isn't it a way of having her back, of wanting to claim her entirely for myself? I fantasize being alive before I was born. How hopeless. One confronts the absence of self, and such a loss is without sweetness, for it is absolute, for no revision is possible. So my mother stares at the camera, which was probably held by her father. She smiles alluringly. She is at that moment a trusting subject. It is a sunny, cloudless day in Miami. But fifty-eight years later a shadow hovers over that moment of bright, familial equilibrium. It is I, it is the future, experiencing a terrible, ineradicable exclusion.

III / ON THE DIFFERENCE BETWEEN FAMILY PHOTOS AND PHOTOS OF THE REST OF THE WORLD

Something about family snapshots sets them apart from photographs of the rest of the world. We look at them differently, feel more passionately about them. They may be of ourselves, no doubt contributing to our greater absorption, but they don't have to be. They can be of anybody we are close to, close enough to so that our emotional ties and shifting affections easily cloud or color our vision of them, leaving us in perpetual doubt as to how they should be seen and making us question whatever views of them we encounter. Family snapshots offer us something like what the French critic Roland Barthes called *punctum*. A punctum is something in the photograph, a detail, that stings or pierces the viewer into an emotional reassessment of what he has seen. It can be a necklace, a flawed smile, the position of a hand—a thing or gesture—that urges itself on us, compels our vision, with sudden, unexpected poignancy. It is not something that can be controlled or anticipated by the photographer, for it is a detail that puts the photograph into a context other than that of its inception. What we experience looking at family snapshots may not be, strictly speaking, what Barthes meant by punctum, but it is related. For often enough we are struck by something in the look of someone we're close to that might tell us more about them and might challenge or confirm the accuracy of our feelings. And often enough the volatility of our needs and expectations changes what we see, turning the images of loved ones into occasions for reverie and the events surrounding them into topics for investigation.

I was being, I admit, a little mischievous when I used the expression "photographs of the rest of the world." After all, the world is large and at least as various as the photographs taken of it. And when I set family snapshots against photographs of the rest of the world, I was creating categories that are based on extremes of experience. I assumed that photographs of the rest of the world do not relinquish themselves to our emotional keep as easily as family pictures. For one thing, we care less about the world than about what

✓

goes on at home; for another, we are able to cast ourselves at the center of our domestic scene, but it would be madness to imagine ourselves at the center of the larger one. When confronted with images of the world, we are rarely stung into revisions and reassessments of ourselves in relation to it. We rarely feel the need to come to terms with what already seems fixed or seems understood, however exotic it might be. Our response is likely to be one of passive acceptance. And the visual climate or character of the photograph will prove subservient to a coding that is culturally or historically determined. Even if the photograph reveals terrible social ills, it will not appear unaccountably problematical; instead, it will inevitably provide an allegorical reading to explain itself. Good and evil will be righteously "exposed," and the photograph's appeal, ultimately, will be to our understanding. In other words, such photographs supply a familiar context by which they can be read. The *unaccounted for*, which in family snapshots often amounts to revelation, is merely out-of-place in photographs of the world.

✓ IV / ON POSING AS A DEFENSE AGAINST THE
CANDOR OF FAMILY PHOTOGRAPHS

Like photos of the rest of the world, formal photographs, or those in which people pose, resist the kind of personal revelation that family snapshots offer. In fact, it could be said that it is precisely personal revelation against which posing is a defense. The poser wants to transcend the interpersonal climate and context of the family snapshot. He does not want to be discovered as anything other than what he determines. He does not wish to be himself so much as he wishes to be an object; that is, he would rather be judged aesthetically than personally, and the world he would join is the permanent one of art. To look alive, for him, is to look flawed. He has an idea about the way he looks, and he wants it confirmed. So he tries to control the outcome of the picture and to anticipate, as much as he can, what he will look like. But his extreme self-consciousness always results in an image of estrangement—a look of dispassion clouds the eyes, he appears to be elsewhere. His expectations are based on delusive claims that have to do with needs beyond the camera's power to satisfy. For instance, if our poser is haunted by conventional beauty, he may wish to look like a movie star; if he is transported by standard embodiments of responsibility, he may wish to look like a statesman. The point is that he wants the camera to be responsive to an image, not to a self.

So what is the poser afraid of? Why does he wish to appear a particular way and not any old way? Is it just vanity that would have him look perfect instead of himself? Or do his needs have more to do with self-preservation; that is, a refusal to be reminded of his mortality? Either way, the results are the same. His idealization means that he will not be located in time. When he looks at the photograph years later, he need not feel even a twinge of sadness, nor need we in the event that our poser has died. We cannot rightly mourn his loss for the simple reason that he has not allowed enough of himself in the photograph. He has become his own ageless memorial.

V / ON RILKE'S POEM "PORTRAIT OF MY FATHER AS A YOUNG MAN": EVIDENCE OF THE LIMITATIONS OF POSING

When I look at the photograph of my mother and grandmother, I experience a sadness that has to do with my own absence from a period of my mother's life. In other words, I experienced my death in reverse—I was born too late to be there. In Rilke's poem "Portrait of My Father as a Young Man," the painstaking scrutiny of a photograph leads the speaker inescapably to a sense of his own mortality.

Portrait of My Father as a Young Man

In the eyes: dream. The brow as if it could feel
something far off. Around the lips, a great
freshness—seductive, though there is no smile.
Under the rows of ornamental braid
on the slim Imperial officer's uniform:
the saber's basket-hilt. Both hands stay
folded upon it, going nowhere, calm
and now almost invisible, as if they
were the first to grasp the distance and dissolve.
And all the rest so curtained with itself,
so cloudy, that I cannot understand
this figure as it fades into the background—.

Oh quickly disappearing photograph
in my more slowly disappearing hand.

Tr. Stephen Mitchell

Those hands folded upon the basket-hilt that will go nowhere, that will complete no gesture—neither in the photograph, because it is still, nor in life because the father is dead—are calm as they disappear. They form a kind of retreat from activity, from actuality. The photograph is fading: everything it pictures is so curtained with itself, so removed, it becomes not a moment that has been rescued but an emblem of death. And as if he could anticipate this at the time the photo was taken, feel the moment of disintegration approaching, Rilke's father already had begun to disengage himself from the inevitable, and substitute another remoteness, one generated from within, the dream whose origins and destiny are more ethereal, harder to pin down than our features. So, even when the photo was taken, he was elsewhere, which is why Rilke has such a hard time locating him. What Rilke encounters in this fading memorial of his father, this mask from which his father had removed himself, is only a pose, which is why he says, "I cannot understand this figure." In order to save his father, he must read into the photograph what it fails to show. Thus "the brow *as if* it could feel something far off," and "the hands *as if* they could grasp [that is, close around, as well as understand] the distance." A photograph cannot describe what is not there. But language can, and this is one of the moving features of Rilke's poem—the desire to know more than the photograph can possibly record, and the ultimate dependence on the speculative properties of language to supply it. Language responds to what is within or behind or hidden, to what, in other words, is not readily seen, suggesting that just as dark is the beginning of invention, so light is its conclusion. Thus, as the light of the photo fades, the poem takes over. And if the hand is a metonym for writing, as it frequently is, then in this poem it assumes the burden of carrying on, for a while, the image of Rilke's father. But only for a while, since the poem, too, is mortal.

VI / ON JOHN ASHBERY'S POEM "MIXED FEELINGS" AND ITS REJECTION OF THE SORT OF SADNESS OFTEN ASSOCIATED WITH FAMILY SNAPSHOTS

John Ashbery's poem begins, as Rilke's does, with the description of a photograph so faded that it is hard to make out. The urgency and tenderness of Rilke's poem concludes rather darkly with an avowal of the poet's own mortal presence. Ashbery's poem takes a different route; resisting any suggestion of darkness, it ends with an assertion of poetic possibility.

Mixed Feelings

A pleasant smell of frying sausages
Attacks the sense, along with an old, mostly invisible
Photograph of what seems to be girls lounging around
An old fighter bomber, circa 1942 vintage.
How to explain to these girls, if indeed that's what they are,
These Ruths, Lindas, Pats and Sheilas
About the vast change that's taken place
In the fabric of our society, altering the texture

Of all things in it? And yet
They somehow look as if they knew, except
That it's so hard to see them, it's hard to figure out
Exactly what kind of expressions they're wearing.
What are your hobbies, girls? Aw nerts,
One of them might say, this guy's too much for me.
Let's go on and out, somewhere
Through the canyons of the garment center
To a small café and have a cup of coffee.
I am not offended that these creatures (that's the word)
Of my imagination seem to hold me in such light esteem,
Pay so little heed to me. It's part of a complicated
Flirtation routine, anyhow, no doubt. But this talk of
The garment center? Surely that's California sunlight
Belaboring them and the old crate on which they
Have draped themselves, fading its Donald Duck insignia
To the extreme point of legibility.
Maybe they were lying but more likely their
Tiny intelligences cannot retain much information.
Not even one fact, perhaps. That's why
They think they're in New York. I like the way
They look and act and feel. I wonder
How they got that way, but am not going to
Waste any more time thinking about them.
I have already forgotten them
Until some day in the not too distant future
When we meet possibly in the lounge of a modern airport,
They looking as astonishingly young and fresh as when this
    picture was made
But full of contradictory ideas, stupid ones as well as

Worthwhile ones, but all flooding the surface of our minds
As we babble about the sky and the weather and the
   forests of change.

So one experiences the gradual wearing away of the already old, mostly invisible photograph of some girls lounging around a fighter bomber in 1942. The process of wearing away is carried on by the continual subversion not only of the photographic image but of what it stands for. First, the girls cannot be aware of the vast changes that have taken place since they were photographed, so whatever claims they might have on the present in which they are being viewed are undermined. Their expressiveness can also be discounted because their faces are difficult to make out. The poet, at a loss as to how to approach the girls, asks a silly question about what hobbies they have. The girls want to get away from this most unhip of voyeurs to a place that is clearly not in the photograph. And he's not offended. Why should he be? He's the source for whatever they do. We might consider the imagined resistance of the girls as part of the complicated flirtation that enables poems to be written. For how can these girls, having no wills of their own and such tiny intelligences, really resist? If they think they're in New York, it's because the poet wants them there—where the poem is. And once he has them there, far from the California climate of the photograph, he can forget them until the possibility arises of using them again. And when that happens, it will be in a thoroughly poetic context, one that is not so emphatically temporal as the photograph, and that will allow them to exist with their youth and vitality restored. They will be full of contradictory ideas, flooding the surface of their minds and the mind of which they are a part—the poet's mind—as they babble about the sky and the weather and the forests of change—stock items, down to the plangency of the final metaphor in the life of most lyric poems. So, the best is yet to come. At least, that's what we are led to believe. For doesn't the poem shift our attention from the inevitable death (by fading) of the photograph to the future, which will be a poem? "Mixed Feelings" began by looking back and ends by looking ahead. It represents a refusal to mourn—not just the passing of four girls or the era they represent, but anything at all. It says *no* to the conventional claims of photography—that "they" (the photographic subjects) are changed or gone—that those who were young and happy are now, alas, old or dead. Its upbeat ending is not an expected response or even, many would say, an acceptable one. More and more, the poem seems like a case of somebody's family photo fallen into the wrong hands.

VII / ON CHARLES WRIGHT'S POEM
"BAR GIAMAICA 1959–60":
THE POEM AS PHOTOGRAPH

Ashbery's poem acknowledges the gratuitous and arbitrary existence of an exploitable photo with the same offhandedness that it takes notice of sausages frying. Charles Wright's poem "Bar Giamaica 1959–60" is saturated with the sort of sadness I have associated with family photographs. It draws

its emotional power not by compensating for photography's
limitations but by identifying with it.

Bar Giamaica 1959–60

Grace is the focal point,
                              the tip ends of her loosed hair
Like match fire in the back light,
Her hands in a "Here's the church. . . ."
                                        She's looking at Ugo Mulas,
Who's looking at us.

Ingrid is writing this all down, and glances up, and stares
            hard.

This still isn't clear.

I'm looking at Grace, and Goldstein and Borsuk and
            Dick Venezia
Are looking at me.

                              Yola keeps reading her book.
And that leaves the rest of them: Susan and Elena and
            Carl Glass.

And Thorp and Schimmel and Jim Gates,
                              and Hobart and Schneeman
One afternoon in Milan in the late spring.

Then Ugo finishes, drinks a coffee, and everyone goes
            away.

Summer arrives, and winter;
>   the snow falls and no one comes back

Ever again,
>   all of them gone through the star filter of memory,
> With its small gravel and metal tables and passers by . . .

An image, a kind of family photograph, is put together before our eyes, and despite all the looking that takes place within the poem, nothing is clear until everyone is accounted for. Then, and only then, can the season and the place be named. The focus or clarity of the poem coincides with the sudden inclusion of the event in time. The poem celebrates the sad moment when we become history—the photographic moment, the moment written about, the moment when everyone goes away, when everyone suddenly ceases to be what they were. Of course, the world goes about its business as it has to: seasons follow, life goes on, the participants in the little party go their separate ways, never to reconvene, not in the world, nor in the poet's imagination—that star filter of memory, with its small metal tables and passersby. The image is forlorn, even grave, and, with the mention of passersby, it does the extraordinary: it enacts its own forgetability, taking a last look at itself. But the moment of loss, which hovered at the fine edge of oblivion, is saved. The poem says what most photographs that commemorate moments say, and what John Ashbery, in "Mixed Feelings" at least, resists saying. That is: "They were here, you can see they were here, and now they're gone." But beyond that, because it ends with an ellipsis, it suggests that an empty stage, with its props (the tables and passersby), waits to be filled, that another reunion, another convening of elements from the past, will take place, and another poem will be written.

The Rilke and the Ashbery poems assume the burden of completing or continuing what was begun in a photograph. Charles Wright's poem is a slightly different case since it never tells us that it is based on a photo. Rather, the poem constructs a photograph as it proceeds, so that it may affect us as photographs do. It even fades at the end, as if to make way for itself—the poem that it is, and the poem that it will be.

On Becoming a Poet

"You, Andrew Marvell" by Archibald MacLeish was the first poem about which I felt passionate, the first that I thought I understood, the first that I actually wished I had written. My own poems—the few that I wrote in my adolescence—were feverish attempts to put "my feelings" on paper, and little more. Their importance, at least for me, their only reader, was exhausted by the time they were written. In those days, my life was one of constantly shifting weather, and the world within was rarely in sync with the world without. No wonder the linearity, the cool emotional order of "You, Andrew Marvell" appealed to me.

The poem was saying things that I wished I could say. The same feelings that had troubled me, and whose victim I was, now seemed, coming from the poem, sources of pleasure. When I read it for the first time, I knew little about poetry. I didn't know who Andrew Marvell was, nor did I know where half of the places were that MacLeish mentions. I only knew—what was most important for me then—that I was the figure "face down beneath the sun." I was the one whose consciousness was connected to the nearing of the night, to its shadow creeping always closer. This description of the distant night's inevitable approach, even as it reflected my own increasing awareness of mortality, was calming. I now felt located in a vastness, which, in my real life, had made me feel lost. The emotions that overwhelmed my solitude took on a shape, one that I found pleasing no matter how often I returned to it. I had no idea of how the poem accomplished its magic, and somehow, despite my many readings of it, I was never moved to inquire.

You, Andrew Marvell

And here face down beneath the sun
And here upon earth's noonward height
To feel the always coming on
The always rising of the night:

To feel creep up the curving east
The earthly chill of dusk and slow
Upon those under lands the vast
And ever climbing shadow grow

And strange at Ecbatan the trees
Take leaf by leaf the evening strange
The flooding dark about their knees
The mountains over Persia change

And now at Kermanshah the gate
Dark empty and the withered grass

And through the twilight now the late
Few travelers in the westward pass

And Baghdad darken and the bridge
Across the silent river gone .
And through Arabia the edge
Of evening widen and steal on

And deepen on Palmyra's street
The wheel rut in the ruined stone
And Lebanon fade out and Crete
High through the clouds and overblown

And over Sicily the air
Still flashing with the landward gulls
And loom and slowly disappear
The sails above the shadowy hulls

And Spain go under and the shore
Of Africa the gilded sand
And evening vanish and no more
The low pale light across the land

Nor now the long light on the sea:

And here face downward in the sun
To feel how swift how secretly
The shadow of the night comes on . . .

. . .

It wasn't until years later, after I had written and published my poems, that I took a close look at it. I remember the mesmerizing power its list of places had over me, how it gave grandiose definition to my vague and fugitive thoughts about death and time passing. But what I had experienced this time was something else. I was aware, as I had been in the past, that the poem seemed suspended between times. Only now that suspension seemed to feature a strange circularity, each event marked by a newness but eerily resembling the events that had come before. The trees at Ecbatan shared something with the grasses at Kermanshah and the gulls over Sicily. Beginning with "And" and ending inconclusively with an ellipsis, the poem as a whole hints at this suspended circularity. Not only does the first line begin with an "and," but the second line does as well, so that the poem seems to insist on its own connective character and, moreover, to allude to something that is ongoing, that won't stop: "And here face down beneath the sun / And here upon earth's noonward height . . ." In other words, "You, Andrew Marvell" is both about time and in time, about motion and in motion. It is both linear and circular, and what it suggests is not just the simple diurnal round of night and day, but the more tragic rise and fall of civilizations.

And yet the poem's speaker seems oddly removed from what he describes—not just because he is situated temporally at precisely noon ("earth's noonward height"), but because his feeling is unattached to tense or to personhood. It exists in an overriding infinitive, out of time but responsive to time: "To feel the always coming on / The always rising of the night: // To feel creep up the curving east / The earthly chill of dusk . . ." Just as "and" is used in the first two lines to underscore the additive elements of the poem, so "always" is used in the next two lines to characterize with reasonable insistence what the infinitive "to feel" can embrace, which is to say "everything."

In another significant gesture of encompassment, the poem's first rhyme of "sun" and "on" is also its last rhyme, not only marking the duration of the speaker's attention but bringing the poem around to what feels like an ending, except that here the ending is a reenactment of the beginning. And it is not only the repeated rhyme that accomplishes the poem's circularity, but its minimal punctuation as well. A colon is used twice, once four lines from the beginning and again four lines from the end. In each symmetrical instance, it signals a pause, which will be followed by the additional pause of the stanza break. The lengthening and doubling of the pause helps to emphasize in yet another way the centrality of the infinitive "to feel."

But somehow the urgency that usually attends feeling seems missing. What is suggested, instead, is that "to feel" embodies a temporal character, and though different from the circular, suspended temporality it responds to, it nevertheless appears related to it. Moreover, because of the ambiguous and, I believe, elaborate way "to feel" is presented, the poem appears to be acknowledging a response that we've already had while at the same time urging us to participate in an extended reconstruction of it. To feel the night come, its advent in various and ravishing manifestations, to be swept up in the vastness of time, to feel it all inwardly, face downward in the sun, is what the poem seems to insist on, but with a languor that is in direct contrast to the heated urgency of the lover's speech in Marvell's "To His Coy Mistress." (In that poem, to which this one obviously responds, no dispassionate view of time's devastating power can be enacted. Love, the act of love, the pleasure it seeks might offer the illusion of sidestepping the inevitable, but the lovers cannot stop the sun, all they can do is make it run; that is, make time pass more quickly, join their heat to the sun's heat.) In MacLeish's poem, there is definitely "world enough and time." Its serenity, the casual way it ticks off exotic places, carries with it the implication that there is something beautiful about bending to what is inexorable, and that meditating on one's mortality can seem a form of transcendence.

Another aspect of MacLeish's use of "to feel" is how it internalizes the huge impersonality of time, and how it makes the visual record of ascending night into a private matter instead of simply a geographic one. We are asked to feel the reach of the poem's vision for as long as we can. And this is probably why it appealed to me as a teenager. The experience the poem offered was that of an immense privacy at the center of which was a figure whose imagination provided the purest and most far-reaching provocation for feeling.

I also undoubtedly liked it for its apparent simplicity. I had no idea that a highly sophisticated craftsmanship was responsible for its easeful disclosures, that the virtual absence of punctuation gave it an added fluency, lending its geographical accretions a hypnotic inevitability. I knew that meter was involved in the enchantment I felt, but I didn't know how important its strict maintenance was to the poem's meaning, that keeping time was the surest way the poem had of adhering to its subject, that the pause and stress of its iambic tetrameter line was as sobering and as steady as nightfall.

The poem's lack of punctuation is one of its most pronounced formal features, the one most responsible for its fluency and the casual way its modifiers shift, clinging momentarily to one noun or verb, then joining forces with another, sometimes following, sometimes preceding. This happens most obviously and most strikingly in the second and third stanzas, first with the rhyme word "slow" and then with the oddly reiterated "strange": "To feel creep up the curving east / The earthly chill of dusk and slow / Upon those under lands the vast / And ever climbing shadow grow // And strange at Ecbatan the trees / Take leaf by leaf the evening strange." "Slow" in stanza two is how "the ever climbing shadow grow[s]," but in stanza three it is also how "leaf by leaf" the trees at Ecbatan absorb the evening. The effortless way "and slow" is coupled with "and strange" three lines later might have been compromised into syntactical fussiness had commas been used. And in an equally understated way, "strange" at the end of the second line of stanza three enacts a doubleness that suits its meaning. It seems at first, in a graceful inversion, like a modifier of "evening." But that's only if we place a comma after it. If the comma is placed before it, then it modifies "the flooding dark" in the subsequent line. Not only that, but the "knees" belong to the "trees," as if rhyme, in compensation for the missing punctuation, were assigning meaning. This works if we place a period after "knees," but doing so only forces the next three lines into an implied sentence of disturbing flatness: "The mountains over Persia change // And now at Kermanshah the gate / Dark empty and the withered grass." With a comma after "knees," however, the line would be subordinated to line four of the third stanza, which could end in either a comma or a period.

And one could go on from there, endlessly changing an imaginary punctuation, creating new shades of meaning, new emphases, but it would be fruitless, since the poem works best just as it is. Its ambiguities are essential not only to its fluidity, but to its vast suggestiveness as well. The poem urges us to read its lines one after another without stopping, yet insisting, it seems to me, on the integrity of each. The line, after all, and not the sentence, is its basic unit. It has no sentences other than the ones our playfulness—or, more likely, our insecurity—would have us invent for it.

II

One might think that my ability to analyze and comment on the technique by which "You, Andrew Marvell" asserts its particular hold on the reader would alter my response to the poem. But my response now is pretty much what it was then. I am still that figure face down in the sun. The experience of the poem has somehow overcome the poem's message of mutability. And the sense that I am still myself—myself essentially as I was—is as present as the knowledge of how swift, how secretly the shadow of the night comes on. It is as if the poem's power to enchant carried with it an obligation to reassure.

Something beyond knowledge compels our interest and our ability to be moved by a poem. As an adolescent, I may not have known anything about the intricacies of poetry, but I was beginning to think about mortal matters the way an adult does. And that more than anything made it possible for me to respond to "You, Andrew Marvell," and, thereafter, to other lyric poems. When I say "lyric poems," I mean poems that manifest musical properties, but are intended to be read or spoken, not sung. They are usually brief, rarely exceeding a page or two, and have about them a degree of emotional intensity, or an urgency that would account for their having been written at all. At their best, they represent the shadowy, often ephemeral motions of thought and feeling, and do so in ways that are clear and comprehensible. Not only do they fix in language what is often most elusive about our experience, but they convince us of its importance, even its truth. Of all literary genres, the lyric is the least changeable. Its themes are rooted in the continuity of human subjectivity and from antiquity have assumed a connection between privacy and universality. There are countless poems from the past that speak to us with an immediacy time has not diminished, that gauge our humanness as accurately and as passionately as any poem written today.

It is not difficult to imagine that most people who have lived on this planet have felt in considering the coming of night the advent of their own mortality. And what they felt did not seem bound by the particular century in which they lived. It is clear that Archibald MacLeish was bound—at least when he was writing this poem—by a notion of time having more to do with the passing of events, human life being one of them, than he was in a theoretical, abstract, or strictly twentieth-century vision of time. For in "You, Andrew Marvell" the earth does not turn. It is darkness that is active. It is darkness that happens to the world just as surely as death will happen to the one face downward in the sun. The poem is bound by a schema that is no less true for standing apart from what science tells us is true. Like most lyrics, it reminds us that we live in time and allows us to feel a certain joy in that knowledge. The losses which are inseparable from experience take on a certain sweetness and resonance.

It is likely that the lyric, either by its formal appeal to memory when rhyme and meter are used, or simply by its being an artifact, provides a redress to its message of human evanescence. "You, Andrew Marvell" is about loss, but the naming of places, even as they fall under the cloak of dark, is an act of restoration. Cities and civilizations are taken away but new ones appear. The ellipsis at the poem's end seems to imply that another cycle of replenishment is on its way; just as the word "always," used with such emphasis at the start of the poem, implies the superabundance and availability of time.

III

It is hard for me to separate my development as a reader of poems from my career as a poet. If my readings have any acuity or sensitivity, it is probably because I have paid such close attention to how my own poems worked, and to which ways and to what extent I might improve them. This mutual dependency is always reflected in the work. A poem will make continual reference to an experience while at the same time call attention to itself as a vehicle for meaning.

Although I no longer wish I had written "You, Andrew Marvell," I wish, however, that I could write something like it, something with its sweep, its sensuousness, its sad crepuscular beauty, something capable of carving out such a large psychic space for itself. It is one of the poems that I read and reread, and that reinforces my belief in poetry, and that makes me want to write. There is something about it that moves me in ways that I don't quite understand, as if it were communicating more than what it actually says. This is often the case with good poems—they have a lyric identity that goes beyond whatever their subject happens to be. They have a voice, and the formation of that voice, the gathering up of imagined sound into utterance, may be the true occasion for their existence. A poem may be the residue of an inner urgency, one through which the self wishes to register itself, write itself into being, and, finally, to charm another self, the reader, into belief. It may also be something equally elusive—the ghost within every experience that wishes it could be seen or felt, acknowledged as a kind of meaning. It could be a truth so forgiving that it offers up a humanness in which we are able to imagine ourselves. A poem is a place where the conditions of beyondness and withinness are made palpable, where to imagine is to feel what it is like to be. It allows us to have the life we are denied because we are too busy living. Even more paradoxically, poetry permits us to live in ourselves as if we were just out of reach of ourselves.

Introduction to
The Best American Poetry 1991

I

It is 1957. I am home on vacation from art school, sitting across from my mother in the living room. We are talking about my future. My mother feels I have picked a difficult profession. I will have to struggle in obscurity, and it may be years and years before I am recognized; even then there is no guarantee that I will be able to make a living or support a family. She thinks it would be wiser for me to become a lawyer or a doctor. It is then that I tell her that although I have just begun art school, I am actually more interested in poetry. "But then you'll *never* be able to earn a living," she says. My mother is concerned that I shall suffer needlessly. I tell her that the pleasures to be gotten from poetry far exceed those that come with wealth or stability. I offer to read her some of my favorite poems by Wallace Stevens. I begin "The Idea of Order at Key West." In a few minutes, my mother's eyes are closed and her head leans to one side. She is asleep in her chair.

II

I do not intend to make fun of my mother. Her failure to respond as I had wished was actually the failing of most people. Hearing poems read, like reading them, is different from other encounters with language. Nothing else we read prepares us for poetry. My mother was a reader of novels and books of general nonfiction. Her responses to what she read were, I believe, knowing and well articulated. But how is poetry different from what she was used to? The difference that comes to mind first is that the context of a poem is likely to be only the poet's voice—a voice speaking to no one in particular and unsupported by a situation or situations brought about by the words or actions of others, as in a work of fiction. A sense of itself is what the poem sponsors, and not a sense of the world. It invents itself: its own necessity or urgency, its tone, its mixture of meaning and sound are in the poet's voice. It is in such isolation that it engenders its authority. A novel, if it is to be believed, must share characteristics with the world we live in. Its people must act in ways we recognize as human, and do so in places and with objects that seem believable. We are better prepared for reading fiction because most of what it tells us is already known. In a poem, most of what is said is neither known nor unknown. The world of things or the world of experience that may have given rise to the poem usually dissolves into the background. It is as if the poem were replacing that world as a way of establishing its own primacy, oddly asserting itself over the world.

What is known in a poem is its language; that is, the words it uses. Yet those words seem different in a poem. Even the most familiar will seem strange. In a poem, each word, being equally important, exists in absolute focus, having a weight it rarely achieves in fiction. (Some notable exceptions can be found in the works of Joyce, Beckett, and Virginia Woolf.) Words in a novel are subordinate to broad slices of action or characterization that push the plot forward. In a poem, they *are* the action. That is why poems establish themselves right away—in a line or two—and why experienced readers of poetry can tell immediately if the poem they are reading possesses any authority. On the other hand, it would be hard for a reader to know much about a novel on the basis of its first sentence. We usually give it a dozen or so pages to earn its right to our attention. And, most often, it has our attention when its language has all but disappeared into the events it generated. We tend to be much more comfortable reading a novel when we don't feel distracted by its language. What we want while reading a novel is to get on with it. A poem works the opposite way. It encourages slowness, urges us to savor each word. It is in poetry that the power of language is most palpably felt. But in a culture that favors speed-reading along with fast food, ten-second news bites, and other abbreviated forms of ingestion, who wants something that makes you slow down?

III

The reading of nonfiction is no greater help than the reading of fiction in preparing one for poetry. Both my parents were avid readers of nonfiction, pursuing information not just for enlightenment but to feel in control of a world they had little say in. Their need for certainty was proportional to their sense of doubt. If one had facts—or what passed for facts—at one's fingertips, one could not only banish uncertainty but also entertain the illusion that one lived in a fixed and static universe, in a world that was passive and predictable and from which mystery was exiled. No wonder poetry was not something my parents found themselves reading for pleasure. It was the enemy. It would only remystify the world for them, cloud certainties with ambiguity, challenge their appetite for the sort of security that knowledge brings. For readers like my parents, poetry's flirtations with erasure, contingency, even nonsense, are tough to take. And what may be still tougher to take is that poetry, in its figurativeness, its rhythms, endorses a state of verbal suspension. Poetry is language performing at its most beguiling and seductive while being, at the same time, elusive, even seeming to mock one's desire for reduction, for plain and available order. It is not just that various meanings are preferable to a single dominant meaning; it may be that something beyond "meaning" is being communicated, something that originated not with the poet but in the first dim light of language, in some period of "beforeness." It may be, therefore, that reading poetry is often a search for the unknown, something that lies at the heart of experience but cannot be pointed out or described without being altered or diminished—something that nevertheless can be contained so that it is not so terrifying. It is not knowledge but rather some occasion for belief, some reason for assent, some avowal of being. It is mysterious or opaque, and even as it invites the reader, it wards him off. This unknown can make him uncomfortable, force him to do things that would make it seem less strange, and this usually means inventing a context in which to set it, something that counteracts the disembodiedness of the poem. As I have suggested, it may have to do with the origin of the poem—out of what dark habitation it emerged. The contexts we construct in our own defense may shed some light, may even explain parts or features of the poem, but they will never replace it in the wholeness of its utterance. Despite its power to enchant, the poem will always resist all but partial meanings.

IV

It could be that my mother, on that day in 1957, sensed this and felt that she was safer within the confines of her own darkness than within the one supplied by Wallace Stevens. But not all poems try to remind us of the dark or the unknown at the center of our experience. Some try not to, choosing to speak of what is known, of common experiences in which our humanness is most powerfully felt, experiences that we share with those who lived hundreds of years ago. It is a difficult task—to speak through the poetic and linguistic conventions of a particular time about that which seems not to have changed. Each poem must, to a certain extent, speak for itself, for its own newness—its ties to and distortions of the conventions of the moment. It must make us believe that what we are reading belongs to us even though we know that what it tells us is really old. This is a form of deception that makes it possible for poetry to escape the commonplace. It is when the conventions of another time, which have been worked and reworked, are used again that we have banality—those tired, sentimental verses, say, that are the stuff of greeting cards. And yet it is precisely through certain vital conventions that we recognize poetry to be poetry. By using old metaphors, recombining them, altering them slightly, by using meters, by re-employing rhyme schemes and stanzaic patterns, fitting them to contemporary speech, its syntax, its idioms, poems pay homage to the poems that preceded them. And this is something that someone unfamiliar with poetry may not know, and on hearing or reading a poem will not catch. This is the secret life of poetry. It is always paying homage to the past, extending a tradition into the present. My mother, who was not a reader of poetry, could not possibly have been aware of this other life of the poem.

V

It is 1965. My mother has died. My first book of poems has been published. My father, who, like my mother, has never been a reader of poems, reads my book. I am moved. The image of my father pondering what I have written fills me with unutterable joy. He wants to talk to me about the poems, but it is hard for him to begin. Finally, he starts. He finds some of the poems confusing and would like me to clarify them. He finds others perfectly clear and is eager to let me know how much they mean to him. The ones that mean most are those that speak for his sense of loss following my mother's death. They seem to tell him what he knows but cannot say. They tell him in so many words what he is feeling. They bring him back to himself. He can read my poems—and I should say that they might have been anyone's poems—and be in possession of his loss instead of being possessed by it.

The way poetry has of setting our internal house in order, of formalizing emotion difficult to articulate, is one of the reasons we still depend on it in moments of crisis and during those times when it is important that we know, in so many words, what we are going through. I am thinking of funerals in particular, but the same is true of marriages and birthdays. Without poetry, we would have either silence or banality, the former leaving us to our own inadequate devices for experiencing illumination, the latter cheapening with generalization what we wished to have for ourselves alone, turning our experience into impoverishment, our sense of ourselves into embarrassment. Had my father lived longer, he might have become a reader of poetry. He had found a need for it—not just a need for my poetry but for the language of poetry, the ways in which it makes sense. And now, even though it is years later, I sometimes think, when I am writing well, that my father would be pleased, and I think, too, that could she hear those lines, my mother would awaken from her brief nap and give me her approval.

Translation

I

A few months ago, my four-year-old son surprised me. He was hunched over, polishing my shoes, when he looked up and said, "My translations of Palazzeschi are going poorly."

I quickly withdrew my foot. "Your translations? I didn't know you could translate?"

"You haven't been paying much attention to me lately," he said. "I've been having a terrible time deciding what I want my translations to sound like. The closer I look at them, the less certain I am of how they are to be read or understood. And since I am just a beginning poet, the more they resemble my poems, the less likely they are to be any good. I work and work, endlessly changing this or that, hoping by some miracle to arrive at just the right rendering of them in an English beyond my abilities to imagine. Oh, Dad, it's been hard."

The vision of my son struggling over Palazzeschi brought tears to my eyes. "Son," I said, "you should find a young poet to translate, someone your own age, whose poems are no good. Then, if your translations are bad, it won't matter."

II

My son's nursery school teacher came over to see me. "I don't know German," she said, as she unbuttoned her blouse and unsnapped her bra, letting them fall to the floor. "But I feel that I must translate Rilke. None of the translations I've read seem very good. If I pooled them, I'm sure I could come up with something better." She dropped her skirt. "I've heard that Rilke is the German Gerard Manley Hopkins, so I'll keep *The Wreck of the Deutschland* on my desk as I work. Some of it is bound to rub off. I'm not sure which poems I'll do, but I favor *The Duino Elegies*, since they are more like my own poems. Of course, I'll be taking German lessons while I work." She took off her panties. "Well," she asked, "what do you think?"

"You are one of those," I said, "who believes translation is a reading not of the original but of every available translated text. Why waste money on German lessons if the actual source of your translation will be already finished translations?" Then, reaching out to shoo a fly from her hair, I said, "Your approach is the editorial one—you edit somebody else's translation until it sounds like yours, bypassing the most important stage in the conversion of one poem to another, which is the initial one of finding rough equivalents, the one which will contain the originality of your reading. Even if you work with someone who knows German, you will be no more than that person's editor, for he will have taken the initial step, and no matter how wisely he rationalizes his choice, it will have been made intuitively or automatically."

"Are you telling me I shouldn't translate?" she said.

III

"What's up?" I said to the nursery school teacher's husband.

"I have decided not to translate in order to save my marriage," he said. "I'd thought of doing Jorge de Lima's poems, but didn't know how." He dabbed his sweaty upper lip with a crumpled hankie. "I thought perhaps that a translation should sound like a translation, reminding the reader that what he was reading had a prior life in another language and was not conceived in English. But I couldn't bring myself to write in a way that would remind somebody that what he was reading was better before I got ahold of it. Dignifying the poem at the cost of the translation seems just as perverse as erasing the original with a translation. Not only that," he said, this time dabbing my upper lip with his hankie, and brushing my cheek with the back of his hand, "but if the dominant poetic idiom of a period determines how a poem is to be translated (and it usually does), it will also determine which poems should be translated. That is, in a period of muttering plain-style lyrics, Baroque formulations of a performative sort will not be looked on favorably. So what should the translator do? Should he adopt an antique style? Or would that parody the vitality, ingenuity, and period naturalness of the original? Though de Lima is a twentieth-century poet, his brand of modernism is passé, quite out of keeping with the poetry being written today. So far as I can see, there's nothing to be done with his poems." And with that he disappeared down the street.

IV

To get away from all the talk of translation, I went camping by myself in southern Utah, and was about to light the campfire when a bare-chested man crawled out from the tent next to mine, stood, and started to file his nails. "You don't know who I am," he said, "but I know who you are."

"Who are you?" I asked.

"I'm Bob," he said. "I spent the first twenty years of my life in Pôrto Velho, and feel that Manuel Bandeira is the great undiscovered twentieth-century poet—undiscovered, that is, by the English-speaking world. I want to translate him." Then he narrowed his eyes. "I teach Portuguese at Southern Utah State where the need for Portuguese is great since so few people there seem to know it exists. You're not going to like this, but I don't go in for contemporary American poetry and don't see why that should disqualify me from translating. I can always get one of the local poets to look over what I've done. For me, meaning is the important thing."

Stunned by his penciled-in eyebrows and tiny mustache, I said, a bit unfairly, "You language teachers are all alike. You possess a knowledge of the original language and, perhaps, some knowledge of English, but that's it. The chances are your translations will be word-for-word rendering without the character or feel of poetry. You are the first to declare the impossibility of translating, but you think nothing of minimizing its difficulty." And with that I packed my things, struck the tent, and drove back to Salt Lake City.

V

I was in the bathtub when Jorge Luise Borges stumbled in the door. "Borges, be careful!" I yelled. "The floor is slippery and you are blind." Then, soaping my chest, I said, "Borges, have you ever considered what is implicit in a phrase like 'I translate Apollinaire into English' or 'I translate de la Mare into French': that we take the highly idiosyncratic work of an individual and render it into a language that belongs to everyone and to no one, a system of meanings sufficiently general to permit not only misunderstandings but to throw into doubt the possibility of permitting anything else?"

"Yes," he said, with an air of resignation.

"Then don't you think," I said, "that the translation of poetry is best left to poets who are in possession of an English they have each made their own, and that language teachers, who feel responsibility to a language not in its modifications but in its monolithic entirety, make the worst translators? Wouldn't it be best to think of translation as a transaction between individual idioms, between, say, the Italian of D'Annunzio and the English of Auden? If we did, we could end irrelevant discussions of who has and who hasn't done a correct translation."

"Yes," he said, seeming to get excited.

"Say," I said. "If translation is a kind of reading, the assumption or transformation of one personal idiom into another, then shouldn't it be possible to translate work done in one's own language? Shouldn't it be possible to translate Wordsworth or Shelley into Strand?"

"You will discover," said Borges, "that Wordsworth refuses to be translated. It is you who must be translated, who must become, for however long, the author of *The Prelude*. That is what happened to Pierre Menard when he translated Cervantes. He did not want to compose another *Don Quixote*— which would be easy—but *the Don Quixote*. His admirable ambition was to produce pages which would coincide— word for word and line for line—with those of Miguel de Cervantes. The initial method he conceived was relatively simple: to know Spanish well, to re-embrace the Catholic faith, to fight against the Moors and Turks, to forget European history between 1602 and 1918, and to *be* Miguel de Cervantes. To compose *Don Quixote* at the beginning of the seventeenth century was a reasonable, necessary, and perhaps inevitable undertaking; at the beginning of the twentieth century it was almost impossible."

"Not almost impossible," I said, "but absolutely impossible, for in order to translate one must cease to be." I closed my eyes for a second and realized that if I ceased to be, I would never know. "Borges . . ." I was about to tell him that the strength of a style must be measured by its resistance to translation. "Borges . . ." But when I opened my eyes, he, and the text into which he was drawn, had come to an end.

Dinner:
Beyond Minimalism,
Beyond Realism,
Beyond Modernism

There was a poets' dinner the other night during which many things said would be forgotten. No one talked about history, though history was alluded to in certain accusations of a personal nature, such as "your work will be forgotten." No one mentioned politics, though the politics of publication did come up in certain pitiful ways, such as "I never get published because nobody likes me." The future was discussed briefly but no conclusions were drawn. No one talked about psychology, which was a surprise, but somebody did say, "Regaining unconsciousness is every writer's dream." And someone in the middle of a story said, "The man screamed and spotted cows on the valley floor bellowed their support." Pakistan was mentioned only once, when a poet said, "A long time ago I took a walk and noticed the moon resting its round chin on the topmost garden stair, it seemed to be saying, 'oh oh.' This was in Lahore." At the other end of the table, somebody said, "Conventions were never intended to hurt anyone; people who hate them want

59

to experience the pain of disbelief." Someone else said, "Catastrophe in a certain high-rent district has taken the life of a princess." Then somebody said, "It might happen, might happen that this is a dinner party, one with a speech, a short speech at the end or near the end," and he got up and said:

"I see I am to give a speech, a short speech. And it would seem by the note printed on our place cards that the title is "Beyond Minimalism, Beyond Realism, Beyond Modernism: The Writing of This Decade." In other words I am to describe the writing of this decade by what it has outgrown or left behind. The title suggests we live in a state of beyondness, a state yet to be named, and so it is up to me, I suppose, to name it and reveal finally where we are. So I find myself in the odd position of describing our situation by predicting what it might be. But because I am not a Christian or a fortune teller, I cannot say what is beyond me. A Christian, of course, would propose that heaven, that airy maximalism, lies beyond. A fortune teller, not having the Christian's need for redress, nor his certainty that "less" at a terminal instant will quickly transform itself into "more," will say only that what lies beyond is "next," any description of which will be a vague version of what went before. But if I didn't have to imagine this decade, I'd say that not much in it has changed from the previous one, and that whatever minimalism, realism, modernism we had then still flourish. This view might be attributable to routine selfishness. Most of us hate the passing of anything with which we have been identified, so we find ways of extending it. To look beyond us is an intolerable thought. We can only hope that beyond us will be nostalgia for us and that we will be reinvented along with our devotions and dogmas. The alternative is frightening. Beyond minimalism—whatever is left of it at any one time—is nothing, for isn't nothing the logical extension of less? And isn't nothing what lies beyond realism, despite realism's self-validating accretions? After all, it is nothing that comes of trying to duplicate the world. (The world's end should now be a familiar enough possibility.) And modernism? Nothing lies beyond it, either. It has perpetuated itself, so far, with such protean vigor that it can look like whatever exists. And if whatever exists ceases—well, then, we have nothing. So it's a choice: we perpetuate ourselves in the name of beyondness or we have a beyond without us. I may sound as if I favor the former, but in fact I find greater consolation in the latter. Thank you very much."

Crumpled napkins were strewn across the table, crumbs and place cards littered the floor, the hosts had gone to bed, the guests had drifted into the night air, the wind howled and howled. The stars were everywhere.

✓

Narrative Poetry

Yesterday at the supermarket, I overheard a man and a woman discussing narrative poetry. She said: "Perhaps all so-called narrative poems only point out how impoverished we are, how, like hopeless utopians, we live for the end. They show that our lives are invalidated by needs, especially the ✓ need to continue. I've come to believe that narrative is born of self-hatred."

He said: "What concerns me is the narrative poem that provides no coherent framework for measuring temporal or spatial passage, the narrative poem in which the hero travels, believing he goes forward when in fact he stands still, becoming the embodiment of narrative poetry, its terrible delusion, the nightmare of its own unreality." ✓

I wanted to remind them that the narrative poem takes the place of an absent narrative and is always absorbing the other's absence so that it can be named, and, at the same time, relinquishing its own presence to the awful solitudes of forgetfulness. The absent narrative is the one, I wanted to say, in which our fate is written. But they had gone before I could speak.

When I got home, my sister was sitting in the living room waiting for me. I said to her: "You know, Sis, it occurred to me that some narrative poems move so quickly they can't be kept up with, and their progress must be imagined. They are the most lifelike and least real." "Yes," said my sister, "but has it occurred to you that some narrative poems move so slowly we are constantly leaping ahead of them, imagining what they might be?" "Yes," I said, "it has occurred to me."

Later, I remembered the summer in Rome when I was convinced that narrative poems in which memory plays a part are self-defeating. Memory, I realized, is a memorial to events that could not sustain themselves into the present, which is why it is tinged with pity and its music always a dirge.

Then the phone rang. It was my mother calling to ask what I was doing. I told her I was working on a negative narrative poem, one that refuses to begin because beginning is meaningless in an infinite universe, and refuses to end for the same reason. It is all a suppressed middle, an inexhaustible conjunction. "And, Mom," I said, "it refuses to mask the essential and universal stillness, and so confines its remarks to what never happens."

. . .

Then my mother said: "Your dad used to talk to me about narrative poetry. He said it was a woman in a long gown who carried flowers. Her hair was red and fell lightly over her shoulders. He said narrative poetry happened usually in spring and involved a man. The woman would approach her house, wave to the man, and drop her flowers. This," Mom continued, "seemed a sign of narrative poetry's point-lessness."

"But Mom," I said, "what we call narrative is simply submission to the predicate's insufferable claims on the future; it furthers continuance, blooms into another predicate. Don't you think that notions of closure rest on our longing for a barren predicate!" "You're absolutely right," said my mother, "there's no other way to think of it." And she hung up.

Notes on the Craft of Poetry

For some of us, the less said about the way we do things the better. And I for one am not even sure that I have a recognizable way of doing things, or if I did that I could talk about it. I do not have a secret method of writing, nor do I have a set of do's and don'ts. Each poem demands that I treat it differently from the rest, come to terms with it, seek out its own best beginning and ending. And yet I would be kidding myself if I believed that nothing continuous existed in the transactions between myself and my poems. I suppose this is what we mean by craft: those transactions that become so continuous we not only associate ourselves with them but allow them to represent the means by which we make art. But since they rarely declare themselves in procedural terms, how do we talk about them? To a large extent, these transactions I have chosen to call craft are the sole property of the individual poet and cannot be transferred to or adopted by others. One reason for this is that they are largely unknown at the time of writing and are discovered afterwards, if at all.

. . .

One essay that had great importance for me when I began to write was George Orwell's "Politics and the English Language." Reading it, I encountered for the first time a moral statement about good writing. True, Orwell was not considering the literary use of language, but language as an instrument for expressing thought. His point was that just as our English can become ugly and inaccurate because our thoughts are foolish, so the slovenliness of our language makes it easier for us to have foolish thoughts. The following rules, he explains, can be relied upon when the writer is in doubt about the effect of a word or phrase and his instinct fails him.

1. Never use a metaphor, simile or other figure of speech which you are used to seeing in print.
2. Never use a long word where a short one will do.
3. If it is possible to cut a word out, always cut it out.
4. Never use the passive where you can use the active.
5. Never use a foreign phrase, a scientific word or jargon word if you can think of an everyday English equivalent.
6. Break any of these rules sooner than say anything outright barbarous.

These are of course very elementary rules and you could, as Orwell admits, keep all of them and still write bad English, though not as bad as you might have. But how far will they take us in the writing of a poem? And how much of that transaction I mentioned earlier is described by them? If following a simple set of rules guaranteed the success of a poem, poems would not be held in very high esteem, as, of course, they are. And far too many people would find it easy to write them, which, naturally, is not the case. For the poems that are of greatest value are those that inevitably, unselfconsciously break rules, poems whose urgency makes rules irrelevant.

I believe that all poetry is formal in that it exists within limits, limits that are either inherited by tradition or limits that language itself imposes. These limits exist in turn within the limits of the individual poet's conception of what is or is not a poem. For if the would-be poet has no idea what a poem is, then he has no standard for determining or qualifying his actions as a poet; i.e., his poem. "Form," it should be remembered, is a word that has several meanings, some of which are near opposites. Form has to do with the structure or outward appearance of something, but it also has to do with its essence. In discussions of poetry, form is a powerful word for just that reason: structure and essence seem to come together, as do the disposition of words and their meanings.

It hardly seems worthwhile to point out the shortsightedness of those practitioners who would have us believe that the form of the poem is merely its shape. They argue that there is formal poetry and poetry without form—free verse, in other words; that formal poetry has dimensions that are rhythmic or stanzaic, etc., and consequently measurable, while free verse exists as a sprawl whose disposition is arbitrary and is, as such, nonmeasurable. But if we have learned anything from the poetry of the last twenty or thirty years, it is that free verse is as formal as any other verse. There is ample evidence that it uses a full range of mnemonic devices, the most common being anaphoral and parallelistic structures, both as syntactically restrictive as they are rhythmically binding. I do not want to suggest that measured verse and free verse represent opposing mnemonics. I would rather we considered them together, both being structured or shaped and thus formal, or at least formal in outward, easily described ways.

Form is manifested most clearly in the apparatus of argument and image or, put another way, plot and figures of speech. This aspect of form is more difficult to discuss because it is less clear-cut; it happens also to be the area in which poems achieve their greatest individuality and where, as a result, they are more personal. This being the case, how is it possible to apply ideas of craft? Well, we might say that mixed metaphors are bad, that contradictions, unless they constitute intentional paradox, must be avoided, that this or that image is inappropriate. All of which is either too vague, too narrow, or mostly beside the point—although there are many creative-writing teachers who have no difficulty discussing these more variable and hidden characteristics of form. And I use the word "hidden" because somehow, when we approach the question of what a poem means, we are moving very close to its source or what brought it into being. To be sure, there is no easy prescription, like George Orwell's, of what to say and what not to say in a poem.

. . .

In discussing his poem "The Old Woman and the Statue,"
Wallace Stevens said:

> While there is nothing automatic about the poem,
> nevertheless it has an automatic aspect in the sense
> that it is what I wanted it to be without knowing before
> it was written what I wanted it to be, even though I
> knew before it was written what I wanted to do.

This is as precise a statement of what is referred to as "the
creative process" as I have ever read. And I think it makes
clear why discussions of craft are at best precarious. We
know only afterwards what it is we have done. Most poets, I
think, are drawn to the unknown, and writing, for them, is a
way of making the unknown visible. And if the object of
one's quest is hidden or unknown, how is it to be
approached by predictable means? I confess to a desire to
forget knowing, especially when I sit down to work on a
poem. The continuous transactions of craft take place in the
dark. Jung understood this when he said: "As long as we ourselves are caught up in the process of creation, we neither
see nor understand; indeed we ought not to understand, for
nothing is more injurious to immediate experience than
cognition." And Stevens, when he said: "You have somehow
to know the sound that is the exact sound: and you do in fact
know, without knowing how. Your knowledge is irrational."
This is not to say that rationality is wrong or bad, but merely
that it has little to do with the making of poems (as opposed,
say, to the understanding of poems). Even so rational a figure as Paul Valéry becomes oddly evasive when discussing

the making of a poem. In his brilliant but peculiar essay "Poetry and Abstract Thought," he says the following:

> I have . . . noticed in myself certain states which I may well call *poetic*, since some of them were finally realized in poems. They came about from no apparent cause, arising from some accident or other; they developed according to their own nature, and consequently I found myself for a time jolted out of my habitual state of mind.

And he goes on to say that "*the state of poetry* is completely irregular, inconstant, and fragile, and that we lose it, as we find it, by accident," and that "a poet is a man who, as a result of a certain incident, undergoes a hidden transformation." At its most comic, this is a Dr. Jekyll/Mr. Hyde situation. And I suppose at its most tragic it still is. But it is astonishing that craft, even in such a figure as Valéry, is beside the point. One feels that Valéry, if given more time, might have become more like Bachelard, who said among other things that "intellectual criticism of poetry will never lead to the center where poetic images are formed."

And what does craft have to do with the formation of poetic images? What does it have to do with the unknown sources of a poem? Nothing. For craft, as it is taught and discussed, functions clearly only if the poem is considered primarily as a form of communication. And yet it is generally acknowledged that poetry invokes aspects of language other than that of communication, most significantly as a variation, though diminished, of a sacred text. Given such status, a status it has for the poet while he is writing, it is not validated by an appeal to experience but exists autonomously, or as autonomously as history will allow. In his essay "On the Relation of Analytical Psychology to Poetry," Jung comes closest to addressing this issue when he says:

> The work presents us with a finished picture, and this picture is amenable to analysis only to the extent that we can recognize it as a symbol. But if we are unable to discover any symbolic value in it, we have merely established that, so far as we are concerned, it means no more than what it says, or to put it another way, that it *is* no more than what it *seems* to be.

This strikes me as a generous statement, for it allows poems an existence ultimately tautological. On the other hand, Freud, who suggests a connection between daydreams and poems—but does not elaborate—and who addresses himself to the fantasies of the "less pretentious writers of romances, novels and stories," making their works into protracted forms of wish fulfillment, seems most intent on establishing the priority of mental states. But the purpose of the poem is not disclosure or storytelling or the telling of a daydream; nor is a poem a symptom. A poem is itself and is the act by which it is born. It is self-referential and is not necessarily preceded by any known order, except that of other poems.

If poems often do not refer to any known experience, to nothing that will characterize their being, and thus cannot be understood so much as absorbed, how can considerations of craft be applied when they are justified on the grounds that they enhance communication? This is perhaps one of the reasons why most discussions of craft fall short of dealing with the essentials of poetry. Perhaps the poem is ultimately a metaphor for something unknown, its working-out a means of recovery. It may be that the retention of the absent origin is what is necessary for the continued life of the poem as *inexhaustible artifact.* (Though words may represent things or actions, in combination they may represent something else—the unspoken, hitherto-unknown unity of which the poem is the example.) Furthermore, we might say that the degree to which a poem is explained or paraphrased is precisely the degree to which it ceases being a poem. If nothing is left of the poem, it has become the paraphrase of itself, and readers will experience the paraphrase in place of the poem. It is for this reason that poems must exist not only in language but beyond it.

Some Observations of
Aeneid *Book VI*

In Book XI of the *Odyssey*, which takes place in the Underworld, Odysseus embraces the ghost of his mother, Anticlea.

> . . . I bit my lip,
> Rising perplexed, with longing to embrace her,
> And tried three times, putting my arms around her,
> But she went sifting through my hands, impalpable
> As shadows are, and wavering like a dream.
>
> (*Od.* 11.204–08; Fitzgerald)

In Book II of the *Aeneid*, Aeneas embraces his wife Creusa's
ghost in the ruins of their abandoned home in Troy.

> . . . three times
> I tried to put my arms around her neck,
> Three times enfolding nothing, as the wraith
> Slipped through my fingers, bodiless as wind,
> Or like a flitting dream.

ter conatus ibi collo dare bracchia circum;
ter frustra comprensa manus effugit imago,
par levibus ventis volucrique simillima somno.

(*Aen.* 2.792–04; Fitzgerald)

In Book VI of the *Aeneid*, Aeneas embraces Anchises, his
father.

. . . And this his tears brimmed over
And down his cheeks. And there he tried three times
To throw his arms around his father's neck.
Three times the shade untouched slipped through his
     hands,
Weightless as wind and fugitive as dream.

sic memorans largo fletu simul ora rigebat.
ter conatus ibi collo dare bracchia circum;
ter frustra comprensa manus effugit imago,
par levibus ventis volucrique simillima somno.

(*Aen.* 6.699–702; Fitzgerald)

In Canto II of *Purgatory*, Dante embraces his old friend, the
singer Casella.

I saw one of those spirits moving forward
     in order to embrace me — his affection
     so great that I was moved to mime his welcome,

O shades—in all except appearance—empty!
    Three times I clasped my hands behind him and
    as often brought them back against my chest.

Io vidi una di lor trarresi avante
    per abbracciarmi, con si grande affetto,
    che mosse me a far lo somigliante.
Ohi ombre vane, fuor che ne l'aspetto!
    tre volte dietro a lei le mani avvinsi,
    e tante mi tornai con esse al petto.

(*Purg.* 2.76–81; Mandelbaum)

II

Odysseus' embrace of his mother comes after they tell each other what each has been doing. She asks, "Have you not seen your lady in your hall" (*Od.* 11.162). He says that he has not been home yet, and wants to know, from his mother, how things are in Ithaca. She is able to fill him in, despite not having known anything of his whereabouts. When she confesses that it was loneliness for him that killed her, Odysseus embraces her. Too much casual conversation surrounds the embrace for us to feel that it means much to Odysseus. Though he accuses Persephone of setting him up with a hallucination "to make him groan again" (*Od.* 11.214), he easily concludes his conversation with his mother by remarking, "so went our talk" (*Od* 11.225). This Underworld domesticity is convincing and is rich in what it says about Odysseus, but it tends to empty the embrace of resonant meaning. Epic does not allow much time for reflection. No sooner does Odysseus say good-bye to Anticlea's ghost than he turns his attention to interviewing other souls. And then he utters one of the poem's best lines: "Here was a great loveliness of ghosts."

III

Towards the end of Aeneas' account to Dido and her court of his escape from the blazing city of Troy, he talks about losing his wife, Creusa, along the way and doubling back at great risk, at least according to Aeneas, to find her. What he finds when he returns to the palace is her ghost "larger than life" (nota maior imago, *Aen.* 2.773).

> I could feel the hair
> On my head rise, the voice clot in my throat;
> But she spake to ease me out of my fear.

> obstipui, steteruntque comae et vox faucibus haesit.
> tum sic adfari et curas his demere dictis.

> (*Aen.* 2.774–75)

What Creusa does is release Aeneas from any further obligation to her. It is a speech of willing self-erasure:

What's to be gained by giving way to grief
So madly, my sweet husband? Nothing here
Has come to pass except as heaven willed.
You may not take Creusa with you now;
It was not so ordained, nor does the Lord
Of high Olympus give you leave. For you
Long exile waits, and long sea miles to plow.
You shall make landfall on Hesperia
Where Lydian Tiber flows, with gentle pace,
Between rich farmlands, and the years will bear
Glad peace, a kingdom, and a queen for you.
Dismiss these tears for your beloved Creusa.
I shall not see the proud homelands of Myrmidons
Or of Dolopians, or go to serve
Greek ladies, Dardan lady that I am
And daughter-in-law of Venus the divine.
No: the great mother of the gods detains me
Here on these shores. Farewell; cherish still
Your son and mine.

quid tantum insano iuvat indulgere dolori,
o dulcis coniunx? non haec sine numine divum
eveniunt; nec te hinc comitem asportare Creusam
fas, aut ille sinit superi regnator Olympi.
longa tibi excilia et vastum maris aequor arandum,
et terram Hesperiam venies, ubi Lydius arva
inter opima virum leni fluit agmine Thybris:
illic res laetae regnumque et regia coniunx
parta tibi; lacrimas dilectae pelle Creusae.

non ego Myrmidonum sedes Dolopumve superbas
aspiciam aut Grais servitum matribus ibo,
Dardanis et divae Veneris nurus;
sed me magna deum genetrix bis detinet oris.
iamque vale et nati serva communis amorem.

(*Aen.* 2.776–89)

Aeneas to Dido and her court then says,

With this she left me weeping,
Wishing that I could say so many things,
And faded on the tenuous air. Three times
I tried to put my arms around her neck,
Three times enfolded nothing, as the wraith
Slipped through my fingers, bodiless as wind,
Or like a flitting dream.

haec ubi dicta dedit, lacrimantem et multa volentem
dicere deseruit, tenuisque recessit in auras.
ter conatus ibi collo dare bracchia circum;
ter frustra comprensa manus effugit imago,
par levibus ventis volucrique simillima somno.

(*Aen.* 2.790–94)

And that is the end of Creusa. She did her job, allowing
Aeneas to pursue his destiny without having to look back,
which, as it happens, he is in the midst of doing. Her depar-
ture is magnanimous, to say the least, but for all its nobility it

seems too convenient, too subservient to narrative considerations, to be a source of lyric passion. Creusa leaves nothing
in her place; she is absorbed into the destiny of Aeneas. Her
speech is coincident with her disappearance and will never
serve as a memorial. The sublime retrievals of elegy are
absent.

IV

In Canto II of *Purgatory*, a crowd of souls arrives on the
mountain island of purgatory and gathers around Vergil and
Dante, who are watching. One of them moves forward to
embrace Dante, and Dante returns the welcome, but with
disappointing results:

> Three times I clasped my hands behind him and
>   as often brought them back against my chest . . .

> tre volte dietro a lei le mani avvinsi,
> e tante mi tornai con esse al petto.

(Purg. 2.80–81)

Only when the spirit steps back does Dante see that it is his
old friend, the singer and musician Casella. At Dante's
request, he begins to sing, but before he can finish, he and
the other newly arrived spirits are urged on by Cato, the
Guardian of Purgatory, in their climb towards God. Of all
the embraces, we feel this one the least, perhaps because it

is the most accidental. Casella is not a family member and is not central to Dante's own spiritual quest. Whatever power his embrace has comes from the other embraces it calls to mind.

V

In Book V of the *Aeneid,* the floating image of Anchises appears out of the darkness to speak to Aeneas. He advises Aeneas to meet him in the Underworld, where the future of Rome will be revealed. In Book VI, the meeting takes place. Aeneas asks Musaeus, the son of Orpheus, where Anchises is. Musaeus replies,

> . . . none of us
> Has one fixed home. We walk in shady groves
> And bed on riverbanks and occupy
> Green meadows fresh with streams. But if your hearts
> Are set on it, first cross the ridge; and soon
> I shall point out an easy path.
> So saying
> He walked ahead and showed them from the height
> The sweep of shining plain. Then down they went
> And left the hilltops.

> 'nulli certa domus; lucis habitamus opacis,
> riparumque toros et prata recentia rivis
> incolimus. sed vos, si fert ita corde voluntas,

hoc superate iugum, et facili iam tramite sistam.'
dixit, et ante tulit gressum camposque nitentis
desuper ostentat; dehinc summa cacumina linquunt.

(*Aen.* 6.673–78)

This is a brief, disengaged passage, but it establishes an air of
great dignity. An immense space, a pastoral setting of sweep-
ing proportions has been created for what is about to happen. Vergil continues,

> Now Aeneas' father,
> Anchises, deep in the lush green of the valley,
> Had given all his mind to a survey
> Of souls, till then confined there, who were bound
> For daylight in the upper world. By chance
> His own were those he scanned now, all his own
> Descendants, with their futures and their fates,
> Their characters and acts. But when he saw
> Aeneas advancing toward him on the grass,
> He stretched out both his hands in eagerness
> As tears wetted his cheeks.

> At pater Anchises penitus convalle virenti
> inclusas animas superumque ad lumen ituras
> lustrabat studio recolens, omnemque suorum
> forte recensebat numerum, carosque nepotes
> fataque fortunasque virum moresque manusque.
> isque ubi tendentem adversum per gramina vidit

Aenean, alacris palmas utrasque tetendit,
effusaeque genis lacrimae et vox excidit ore.

(*Aen.* 6.679–86)

Anchises turns from this vision to Aeneas, who says,

. . . let me have your hand, let me embrace you,
Do not draw back.

da iungere dextram,
da, genitor, teque amplexu ne substrahe nostro.

(*Aen.* 6.697–98)

Then Vergil, in a passage of extraordinary beauty, describes the embrace of Aeneas and Anchises.

At this his tears brimmed over
And down his cheeks. And there he tried three times
To throw his arms around his father's neck,
Three times the shade untouched slipped through his
     hands,
Weightless as wind and fugitive as dream.
Aeneas now saw at the valley's end
A grove standing apart, with stems and boughs
Of woodland rustling, and the stream of Lethe
Running past those peaceful glades. Around it
Souls of a thousand nations filled the air,
As bees in meadows at the height of summer

Hover and home on flowers and thickly swarm
On snow-white lilies, and the countryside
Is loud with humming. At the sudden vision
Shivering, at a loss, Aeneas asked
What river flowed there and what men were those
In such a throng along the riverside.

sic memorans largo fletu simul ora rigebat.
ter conatus ibi collo dare bracchia circum;
ter frustra comprensa manus effugit imago,
par levibus ventis volucrique simillima somno.
      Interea videt Aeneas in valle reducta
seclusum nemus et virgulta sonantia silvae,
Lethaeumque domos placidas qui praenatat amnem.
hunc circum innumerae gentes populique volabant,
ac velut in pratis ubi apes aestate serena
floribus insidunt variis et candida circum
lilia funduntur, strepit omnis murmure campus.
horrescit visu subito causasque requirit
inscius Aeneas, quae sint ea flumina porro,
quive viri tanto complerint agmine ripas.

(*Aen.* 6.699–712)

Of all the embraces, this one strikes me as the most moving.
It is the only one that accommodates the forward motion of
epic to a vision of pastoral. None of the other embraces
compels our attention the way this one does. In the *Odyssey*,
a brief explanation by Odysseus' mother of what happens
when one dies follows the embrace. This, in turn, is fol-

lowed by the homely injunction to remember to tell Penelope of the strange things he witnessed in the Underworld. The embrace is forgotten, as it is in Book II of the *Aeneid*, where Aeneas turns his attention to his father and to those who have gathered for exile. The event is closed off, an oddity, a near embrace without resonance. In Dante, where so many strange and miraculous things happen, it seems little more than a small detail, a failed attempt at greeting a long-lost friend.

One of the reasons Aeneas' embrace of Anchises achieves greater force is because it is described in the third person. Vergil can place Aeneas in a context that only compounds the failure of the embrace, and he can describe Aeneas, report on what he thinks and says, so that finally Aeneas is contained by the scene. Aeneas does not have to speak. He can be silent and the narrative will continue.

VI

Before I take a closer look at what happens at this point in Book VI, I should make clear the major pitfall of doing so. That is, if one's reading of Vergil depends entirely upon translation, there is only so much that can be assumed about the original. The translator can be trusted to represent the broad features of the *Aeneid*, but when it comes to details upon which a close reading depends, we should be cautious. For instance, can we assume that the slight difference in English between Aeneas' embrace of Creusa and his embrace of Anchises reflects the same difference in Latin?

When Vergil in Book VI says, "the shade untouched slipped through my hands" (ter frustra comprensa manus effugit imago, *Aen.* 6.701), is it really different from Aeneas in Book II reporting that "the wraith slipped through my fingers" (ter frustra comprensa manus effugit imago, *Aen.* 2.793)? Except for the implication that what slips through one's hands may be larger in scale that what slips through one's fingers, there is very little difference. And if we compare the lines that immediately follow, a similar distinction can be observed. In Book II, we have "bodiless as wind, or like a flitting dream" (par levibus ventis volucrique simillima somno, *Aen.* 2.794). Its parallel in Book VI is "weightless as wind and fugitive as dream" (par levibus ventis volucrique simillima somno, *Aen.* 6.702), which is grander, I think, with both attributes laid down in a single line. The quote from Book II offers us one or the other. Not only that, but the word "flitting" *(volucrique)*, though commonly used in antiquity to describe the motions of the soul, does not seem appropriate in our day as a modifier for "dream" *(somno)*, nor does it seem to fit the solemnity of the occasion. Like fingers relative to hands, it seems to diminish the force of what preceded it.

The translation has forced us to question subtleties which do not occur in the original. In Latin, the several lines describing each embrace are identical. So why does Fitzgerald deviate? Did he consider an exact duplication of words inappropriate to the character of each embrace? Did he feel a distinction should be made between the language of Aeneas and that of Vergil? He was not alone in what he chose to do. Dryden did the same, and so did Mandelbaum, and others as well.

VII

When I said earlier that the compound line "weightless as wind and fugitive as dream" (par levibus ventis volucrique simillima somno, *Aen.* 6.702) seemed right for the occasion, I meant that the pastoral scene that follows is, in itself, a compounding of Aeneas' experience of loss. Having embraced the absence of his father, Aeneas now takes in a whole landscape in which "souls of a thousand nations fill the air" (hunc circum innumerae gentes populique volabant, *Aen.* 6.706). They are, he says,

> as bees in meadows in the height of summer
> Hover and home on flowers and thickly swarm
> On snow-white lilies, and the countryside
> Is loud with humming.

> ac velut in pratis ubi apes aestate serena
> floribus insidunt variis et candida circum
> lilia funduntur, strepit omnis murmure campus.

(*Aen.* 6.707–09)

This is both a continuation and a changing of the embrace. The simile performs an act of poetic replenishment. Vergil describes a flourishing of bodilessness. When Aeneas asks Anchises in the lines immediately following—"What river flows there and what men are those in such a throng along the riverside?" (quae sint ea flumina porro, / quive viri tanto complerint agmine ripas. *Aen.* 6.711–12)—the answer

Anchises gives him bears directly upon the regenerative properties of Vergil's evocation of pastoral plenitude. Those gathered at the river are "souls for whom a second body is in store" (animae, quibus altera fato / corpora debentur, *Aen.* 6.713–14). In other words, a new beginning awaits them. This is very different from what happens at the close of Book XI in the *Odyssey*. First, a spectacular image in Fitzgerald's translation tells us that Odysseus' anticipated meeting with some of the great heroes of the past is interrupted by "Shades in thousands, and a pandemonium of whispers, blown together" (*Od.* 11.632–33). Then a terrifying premonition that Persephone is about to bring from darker hell a saurian death's-head has Odysseus running as fast as he can to exit the Underworld and safely board his ship.

VIII

What the embraces have in common is that they signify possession and loss at the same time. And, of course, each embrace is actually three embraces, a fact which, besides the likelihood of its making numerological or mystical sense, makes psychological sense. One attempt at an embrace would be insufficient; a second attempt would merely confirm the strangeness of the first; but a third establishes the utter futility of making further attempts. Anything beyond three would seem either comic or the surreal enactment of repetition-compulsion. Each of the shades is able to speak, and yet each is insubstantial. Each can be moved to tears, tears that we assume are a real manifestation of their joy or sorrow—emotions which we must also suppose are real. Each is an embodiment of speech and feeling, and each might be called, accommodatingly, a figure of speech.

A peculiar doubleness pervades Book VI. Things are present and yet they are not. Vision and action are accorded epic scale, but they hint at the lyric. The future is both itself and the past. Aeneas listens to Anchises but cannot embrace him. The reader reads Book VI but cannot be sure of where Vergil is—he seems as ghostly as Anchises. This suggests that the Underworld and poetry have something in common. When Aeneas, upon hearing from Anchises that the souls he sees will be returning to the body's "dead weight" (tarda corpora, *Aen.* 6.720–21), asks, "How can they crave our daylight?" (quae lucis miseris tam dira cupido, *Aen.* 6.721), he is in fact questioning the wisdom of accepting the prose of everyday life over the magical properties of poetry. But he also knows that the embrace which ended in failure in the world below would have succeeded in the actual world, that corporeality has its dispensations. The spiritual world of poetry and the spiritual world of Hades permit us to see beyond what our bodies can allow, but they do not permit physical participation. The Underworld embrace offers what a poem does, which is the inseparability of presence and bodilessness.

If the description of the embrace of Anchises and Aeneas is more moving than the others I have touched on, it is because of its lyric character. Even the great catalogue of the future, of the glory that will be Rome, ends up sounding more elegiac than epic, more like dirge, a slow parade of mortals "under the great sky" (magnum caeli . . . sub axem,

Aen. 6.790). Whatever is acknowledged or named into being assumes the sad quality of having been. So that near the end of Book VI, when Anchises is so moved by the appearance of young Marcellus that he wishes to scatter lilies and scarlet flowers before him, it is more than anything like the laying down of a wreath. One feels that Rome's past is being memorialized rather than Rome's future celebrated. It is this contradiction which may be at the center of Aeneas' puzzling exit from the Underworld through the gate of ivory, which, as everyone knows, is the gate through which false dreams pass on their way to the world above. Could it be that the sanctity of Anchises' revelation has been compromised by its not being a true revelation and by Aeneas not being a true shade? It is not possible to memorialize what has not happened, nor possible to pass off what has already happened as what will happen. Each alternative is false, which is why Vergil—in what seems like a judgment of himself and his rendering of the existence of Rome—sends Aeneas back to the upper world through the ivory gate. It is the gate, at least in this instance, where prolepsis and prophecy meet, where elegy imagines a future that mourns the past, and epic sacrifices the present to achieve the future. Because we are made to feel, especially in Book VI, epic creating the conditions for elegy, the existence of Rome becomes an occasion for mourning. It is the lyric and not the epic that offers images of continuity which can be set against the fact of mortality.

Introduction to Joseph Brodsky

Recently, in a book review, I read that Joseph Brodsky was becoming an American poet. Well, as nice as that would be for American poetry, it does not seem likely. And I think the reviewer actually was saying that Brodsky had begun to write in English. There is no American poet that Brodsky resembles in the least, and the only recent poet writing in English with whom he can be compared is W. H. Auden. Like Auden, he is a poet who deliberately enunciates his climate of opinion, who feels empowered to make clarifying or didactic statements, and whose consciousness (or rather the consciousness of his poetry) is located almost always within the context of an historical situation. Perhaps more than anything else, it is his relation to history that forces Brodsky into stances common to more than himself, and makes him seem, in his poetry, representative, and lends his poetry an external character. Poets like Auden or Brodsky may present autobiographical detail and may know, as in Auden's case, all one can about *angst*, or as in Brodsky's, all one can about exile, suggesting a tone and character that is personal. Yet both exile and angst for them are essentially thematic properties leading to generalized observations, not to mysterious particulars. Rather than the sufferers of a tradition, they are the custodians of one. This is more Augustan than it is American. No American poet is the clarifier of social attitudes or public feeling. Deeply rooted in the ongoing romance of the self, the American poet could not possibly claim to represent anything more than his biographical existence. Even if he should care about history, it comes out like biography; it is valid only to the degree that it inhabits him. For most American poets, history ceases to be recognizable as anything that has a will and destiny of its own. For Brodsky, it is definitely out there. He records its turnings, its sequences, armed with reason, irony, and a fatalism that is as highly nuanced as it is stubborn.

By making such comparisons, I do not mean to downgrade American poetry. I merely want it understood that there is an essential difference between Brodsky's work and the work that surrounds him in his country of exile. Given the introspective nature of American poetry, Brodsky's world, the world in his poetry, seems large—morally large. His truths seem to have come a more difficult route. His baroque elaborations made with colloquial emphasis are more than exotic, for they convince us that sincerity is not only the property of plain speech or of hours spent talking into a mirror. We also learn from reading Brodsky that nothing can be known finally, but all things exist in a never-ending chain of contexts. This is probably why the world seems so much larger in Brodsky's poetry than it does in anyone else's now writing.

Poetic Justice

Donald Justice's *New and Selected Poems* enacts a brilliant accommodation to almost everyone's expectations of poetry. The poems have a sweet and measured gravity that engages us on a level more profound than the one we usually find ourselves on. His early poems, in their evocation of simpler, though not necessarily better, times, recall John Crowe Ransom: they possess the same detachment, the same mix of elegance and decorum, the same reliance on narrative's charms as opposed to the sudden revelations of figurative language. But Justice's are plainer, less artificial, less given to periphrasis. And they are beautiful in ways that are often difficult to detect. Beyond the rhymes and the shapely stanzas, beyond the slightly rueful tone and the poised insistence on mortal matters, there is something else. They have a modesty—never declared, of course—that is extremely touching and inviting, as well as a hesitancy, accomplished by the use of the word "perhaps" or of a clause whose purpose is to defer the inevitable and give the reader time to savor the poem's tonality, its wit, its particular truth. Take "The Artist Orpheus," where Justice offers an original and brilliant revision of the Orpheus myth. This is the end of it:

He might have sworn that he did not look back,
That there was no one following on his track,
Only the thing was that it made a better story
To say that he had heard a sigh perhaps
And once or twice the sound a twig makes when it snaps.

Deferment of another sort—performative, comic—is carried out in a revision of the poet's traditional dependence on the muse ("The Telephone Number of the Muse"):

Sleepily, the muse to me: "Let us be friends.
Good friends, but only friends. You understand."
And yawned. And kissed, for the last time, my ear.
Who earlier, weeping at my touch, had whispered:
"I loved you once." And: "No, I don't love him,
Not after everything he did." Later,
Rebuttoning her nightgown with my help:
"Sorry, I just have no desire, it seems."

How convincingly this effortless, though syncopated, blank verse becomes plain speech. How easily the poet's commerce with his paramour becomes just another failed sexual escapade. The aging poet's inability to satisfy his muse suggests, naturally, his failing powers as a poet, but never has this been so delicately admitted, so unhistrionically accepted. And the poem ends without a trace of self-pity:

I call her up sometimes, long distance now.
And she still knows my voice, but I can hear,
Beyond the music of her phonograph,

The laugher of the young men with their keys.

I have the number written down somewhere.

In speech that is more elaborate but no less convincing in its claims on our attention, Justice will extend a sentence not only for the pleasure of the rhymes but for the satisfaction of prolonging rapture, rapture that often has a languorous and collected air, as in the opening stanza of "Ode to a Dressmaker's Dummy":

> O my coy darling, still
>   You wear for me the scent
> Of those long afternoons we spent,
>   The two of us together,
> Safe in the attic from the jealous eyes
>   Of household spies
> And the remote buffooneries of the weather;
>   So high,
> Our sole remaining neighbor was the sky,
>   Who, often enough, at dusk
> Leaning her cloudy shoulders on the sill,
> Used to regard us with a bored and cynical eye.

In reading Justice, one feels keenly that a poem is an act of retrieval—that as it memorializes, so it revives. When Justice remembers the thirties, the decade of his youth, it is with a poignancy rarely found in today's poetry. Memory and rapture are so closely intertwined that they become a single gesture of sustained regard. And though an intense

nostalgia is the result, it is held in check by rigorous asser-
tions of limitation, which in themselves give pleasure—the
varied meter, the resourceful rhymes. An instance of this is
his poem "Dance Lessons of the Thirties":

> Wafts of old incense mixed with Cuban coffee
> Hung on the air; a fan turned; it was summer.
> And (of the buried life) some last aroma
> Still clung to the tumbled cushions of the sofa.
>
> At lesson time, pushed back, it used to be
> The thing we managed somehow just to miss
> With our last-second dips and whirls—all this
> While the Victrola wound down gradually.
>
> And this was their exile, those brave ladies who taught us
> So much of art, and stepped off to their doom
> Demonstrating the fox-trot with their daughters
> Endlessly around some sad and makeshift ballroom.
>
> O little lost Bohemias of the suburbs!

Justice's retrievals of lost time are achieved not just by the
shrewd and evocative detail. Most frequently and most spec-
tacularly, he employs the refrain, and the form in which it
occurs with the greatest regularity happens to be the villanelle—a form that Justice has experimented with perhaps
more than any other poet now writing. A villanelle is a
nineteen-line poem in which, among other things, two lines
are used four times. The lines keep coming back at you, cre-

ating a counter-motion, a circularity, in which it is safe to talk about loss, because the feeling one gets reading a villanelle is that nothing is lost. The subject may be ruin—public or private—but the form is all recovery.

The connections Justice makes in his work are not only to his own past but to his literary precursors as well: the Spanish poets Lorca and Alberti, Rilke to a certain extent, Baudelaire to a greater extent, and Yeats. Justice often pays homage to work he admires by writing a poem based on a poem, as in "Invitation to a Ghost," which leans heavily on Alberti's "The Coming Back of an Assassinated Poet." But where Alberti begins his poem by saying (to Lorca) "You have come back to me older and sadder," Justice begins his (to his friend the poet Henri Coulette) "I ask you to come back now as you were in youth."

The major influence, however, has been Wallace Stevens. Sometimes his debt to the Master is acknowledged directly; at others, it is only hinted at, as in "Variations for Two Pianos":

> There is no music now in all Arkansas.
> Higgins is gone, taking both his pianos.
>
> Movers dismantled the instruments, away
> Sped the vans. The first detour untuned the strings.
>
> There is no music now in all Arkansas.
>
> Up Main Street, past the cold shopfronts of Conway,
> The brash, self-important brick of the college,

Higgins is gone, taking both his pianos.

Warm evenings, the windows open, he would play
Something of Mozart's for his pupils, the birds.

There is no music now in all Arkansas.

How shall the mockingbird mend her trill, the jay
His eccentric attack, lacking a teacher?

Higgins is gone, taking both his pianos.
There is no music now in all Arkansas.

Formal elaboration and musical erasure are perfectly balanced in this abbreviated villanelle. Its repetitions, its accretive energies seem to address the removal of the pianos by making a music of their absence. And though the poem is vintage Justice, it reminds one of Stevens's famous poem "Anecdote of the Jar." The comic grandiosity of "I placed a jar in Tennessee" is echoed by "There is no music now in all Arkansas." And the order created by Stevens's placement of the jar contrasts nicely with the disorder left by the removal of Higgins's pianos.

The remarkable feature of Justice's literary dependence is that it is so natural, so unshowy, and so much of a piece with his inclination to feel the exactions of time. He is not an allusive poet, making pointed reference; rather, he absorbs the rhetorical stratagems of others—always, it seems, to meet his purposes, which are to give melancholy a precision without compromising its depth and to make even the most subtle and mysterious of our affections accessible.

Workshop Miracle

(A SHORT OPERA)

Scene: A university classroom.

PROF. SMITH
Jones, did you write a poem today?

JONES
I did.

PROF. SMITH
You did? You, the least promising student in class, wrote a poem? Only under my guidance could such a thing happen. Jones, will you share your poem with us?

JONES
I can't, sir. I haven't got it with me, and since I wrote it in free verse, I can't remember it.

PROF. SMITH
Can you tell us a little about it then?

JONES

Only in rhyme, sir.

PROF. SMITH

Well?

JONES

It says that fields of autumn flowers will not end in frost,
which would be nice, but in a distant smear
of embers drifting everywhere, forever lost.
And farther down, it says much worse,
That those who were not friends on earth
will spend eternity together; the sheep
will ride the whale's great back in the silent deep,
the dog and the hare will swing side by side, year after year;
and then it says that we, no matter what we do,
will not be spared the rushing tides and heavy undertow
of dark. In every verse, one feels the slow
and fated burial of all we know . . .

PROF. SMITH

That will do, Jones. Clara, what do you think of Jones's
work? Not the rhymed paraphrase, of course, but what you
take to be the real thing?

CLARA

May the Muses of Sicily fall to their knees! It is your work,
Professor, that we should applaud. If a poem can be born in
a place like this, poetry will never die. Nor will it want to die,
though I can imagine it will be tempted from time to time.

PROF. SMITH

Oh Clara, as usual, you are right. Let's work together so poetry will never die.

WHOLE CLASS

Together, together, so poetry will never die. Together, together [*etc.*].

Landscape and the
Poetry of Self

When Wordsworth "escaped from the vast city" and embarked on his journey which would be *The Prelude*, he did so with enviable self-assurance, as if he clearly anticipated what was to come.

> I look about, and should the guide I choose
> Be nothing better than a wandering cloud,
> I cannot miss my way.

The sense is that if he were "there," he would find himself and, conversely, if he were "not there," he would be lost. Throughout *The Prelude* there is a presumption about Being that no contemporary poet, so far, has been able to make. It is not merely that Nature is good, that it is "the very shape and quality and image of right reason," but that Being is an adequate reflection of Nature, that, in fact, it is a necessary equal to the power which inspires it and to which it in turn gives poetic life. Wordsworth takes his own Being in the world more for granted than any contemporary poet is able to. Nature will "sanctify," he says, "and purify . . . until we recognize a grandeur in the beatings of the heart." But one feels in *The Prelude* that "the beatings of the heart" were there all the while and that for Wordsworth the self precedes experience. How else is one to explain his assurance? It is this that gives his subjectivity its curious authority and saves it, though not always, from the insecurities which characterize the contemporary poet's efforts to write about himself. For the contemporary poet, experience must precede a sense of self. This is one of the essential differences between *The Prelude* and recent attempts at autobiographical verse, notably *Life Studies* by Robert Lowell and *The Dream Songs* by John Berryman. Perhaps we should observe some contrasts in these opposite modes of autobiographical poetry: the subjective-visionary mode of Wordsworth and the confessional mode of Lowell and Berryman.

In *The Prelude*, the self *is* because it brings itself into being, recalls itself. It emerges from the fabric of the language of retelling. It incorporates, as it were, the very nature that inspires it into being. It makes a silent claim for primacy, and we almost feel that Nature is its invention, or that Nature's self is "by human love assisted," though Wordsworth goes out of his way to deny his work or himself a status equivalent to Nature's:

> . . . the forms
> Of Nature have a passion in themselves
> To which she summons him, although the works
> Be mean. . . .

In most so-called confessional poetry, there is no governing vision of submergence or transcendence as there is in

Wordsworth. Submergence occurs when the poet uses darkness as a medium and communicates with his own unconscious. It is through such process that the poet makes the universe internal until it takes on his form. Transcendence is the process by which the poet puts himself into the universe until he becomes identified, finally, with the divine event. Light is its medium.

In confessional poetry, the self is terminal, physical, isolated, and depends heavily on specific information—the names of friends, doctors, stores, places, and the like. There is a grasping after concrete detail as a way of authenticating the self. It is as if the confessional poet were saying that because he has documentary evidence of his experience, he must therefore exist.

On the other hand, there are few specifics in *The Prelude*. There are major events which are described in some detail, but it is hard to characterize the detail. For these events, which are often scenes or vision-scenes, are too encompassing to be imagistic and too natural to be emblematic. The "green vales," the "lonesome peaks," the "quiet streams" of *The Prelude* serve both as presences and as indicators of a landscape in the poet's previous experience. The descriptions are necessarily generalized, since Wordsworth is attempting to conjure up an entire landscape. Here again, he derives assurance from his having been there before. And he is not making contact with a place so much as he is with the sense of a place. And the sense of place is precisely what he carries with him and has carried since he was a child.

> . . . even then,
> A child, I held unconscious intercourse
> With the eternal Beauty, drinking in
> A pure organic pleasure from the lines
> Of curling mist, or from the level plain
> Of waters colour'd by the steady clouds.

In confessional poetry, the poet is revealed journalistically, not imaginatively. His own mysteriousness, however harmless, is not alluded to, for mystery of any kind is threatening, and the operations of confessional poetry depend on a known universe. The tone is familiar, usually because the situation is local. Of course, not all confessional poets are alike in their employment of concrete detail and specific information. In his book *Life Studies*, Lowell is the model confessional poet. He speaks casually, intimately, in the first person, in a voice that seems more than anything a rhetorical compromise between nostalgia and horror. Berryman, in his *Dream Songs*, is the lunatic fringe of the confessional school—if it is a school. Berryman refuses to have us believe he is Henry, the hero of *The Dream Songs*. For him, obviously, responsibility for being oneself does not begin in dreams, but rather the dream for Berryman is that state where things exist and don't exist, where Henry can be Berryman and Berryman can deny it. Unlike Lowell, Berryman never establishes the content of his confession wholly in the content of his verse. His confession is as much in his manner and in his need for a persona. To a certain extent, Wordsworth's confession or, more precisely, his autobiography exists in the manner of telling it, but no persona is needed in *The Prelude*. Rarely is Wordsworth's confidence shaken. The celebrated "I" easily sustains itself in Nature and does not have to arm itself with a voice tailored to the event. It *is* the event. It is what it says, and as it speaks so is it born. But Berryman does not wish to be so close to himself. As long as he is Henry, he can be weak without being vulnerable. He can gossip, be melodramatic or mawkish, admit frailty with preposterous vanity, but always at one remove from himself. Berryman's confession is the desperate intensity of his pretense. Those mannered, extravagant gestures which seem so remote from their source are ultimately a way of doing the self in. It is a paradox that Berryman's *Dream Songs*, which in their obsessive and drunken way seem so open, so much the spontaneous overflow of social feeling and personal attitude, should result in establishing distance between themselves and the reader. It is a poetry of the self which denies the self. Here is "Dream Song 356."

> With fried excitement he looked across at life
> wondering if he could bear it more,
> wondering,
> in the middle of a short war with his wife,
> deep in the middle, in short, of a war,
> he couldn't say whether to sing
>
> further or seal his lonely throat, give himself up.
> Tomorrow is his birthday, makes you think.
> The London *TLS*
> are mounting só much of him he could scream.
> There was a time he marched from dream to dream
> but he seems to be out of ink,

he seems to be out of everything again
save whiskey & cigarettes, both bad for him.
He clapped both hands to both ears
and resigned from the ranks of giving men.
In a minute now he'll wake, distinct & grim.
I'm not, he cried, what I appears.

Lowell, on the other hand, never questions his being in so fundamental a way. And yet there is enormous tension in his poems. Lowell would like to bury his past, but needs it for the mythologizing of himself. He wavers between family history and history as family. As a consequence, the mythic portentousness of some of his poems is full of self-mocking irony. I shall cite his poem "Terminal Days at Beverly Farms."

At Beverly Farms, a portly, uncomfortable boulder
bulked in the garden's center—
an irregular Japanese touch.
After his Bourbon "old fashioned," Father,
bronzed, breezy, a shade too ruddy,
swayed as if on deck-duty
under his six pointed star-lantern—
last July's birthday present.
He smiled his oval Lowell smile,
he wore his cream gabardine dinner-jacket,
and indigo cummerbund.
His head was efficient and hairless,
his newly dieted figure was vitally trim.

Father and Mother moved to Beverly Farms
to be a two minute walk from the station,
half an hour by train from the Boston doctors.
They had no sea-view,
but the sky-blue tracks of the commuter's railroad shone
like a double-barreled shotgun
through the scarlet late August sumac,
multiplying like cancer
at their garden's border.

Father had had two coronaries.
He still treasured underhand economies,
but his best friend was his little black *Chevie*,
garaged like a sacrificial steer
with gilded hooves,
yet sensationally sober,
and with less side than an old dancing pump.
The local dealer, a "buccaneer,"
has been bribed a "king's ransom"
to quickly deliver a car without chrome.

Each morning at eight-thirty,
inattentive and beaming,
loaded with his "calc" and "trig" books,
his clipper ship statistics,
and his ivory slide rule,
Father stole off with the *Chevie*
to loaf in the Maritime Museum of Salem.
He called the curator
"the commander of the Swiss Navy."

> Father's death was abrupt and unprotesting.
> His vision was still twenty-twenty.
> After a morning of anxious, repetitive smiling,
> his words to Mother were:
> "I feel awful."

The confessional poet's need to document his life with facts gives his poetry a chatty quality. No matter how self-centered the confessional poet is, he is tirelessly sociable. If he does not live in the city proper, then he lives in a place where he seems surrounded by people. For it is social life that provides him with self-authenticating action. Unlike Wordsworth, the confessional poet cannot bear to be alone. His insecurity and his consequent mania for naming keep him from being a truly subjective poet. He names in order to possess, and possessing, in turn, is part of what helps him to account for himself.

In landscape it is important to possess nothing. One does not travel in a landscape with belongings. The traveler in a landscape—for landscape will support no one else—must be willing to lie down at any time under a tree and spend the night, as Wordsworth's model men, the shepherds, do. His spirituality depends on his unencumbered spontaneity and his purity as wanderer.

The subjective poet wishes to be not merely a commentator, a condition which requires distance and objectivity for its success, but rather the maker of the world he lives in. He creates a poetic situation in which the broadest, least limited associations are possible. In this way, he does not have to account for individual objects, nor overcome the resistance of separate destinies. His purpose is to break down the barriers which keep him and the world apart. The dissolution of boundaries means ridding himself of names which already identify, make singular, prevent him from speaking generally—describing the world as an omniscient spirit. One of the results of this is that his world is more permanent. His landscape, half-seen, half-invented, as the sound of Wordsworth's Derwent was "half-heard and half-created," has the endurance of imagination. No things but in ideas—otherwise they will disappear!

Rarely in *The Prelude* does Wordsworth fall into the habit of naming, and when he does, his poem is weakest and takes on some of the shortcomings with which I have characterized our two leading confessional poets. In London and to a certain extent in Cambridge, Wordsworth was not able to find himself. He was not able to absorb or to take in London's vast and changeable nature. His experience there is not ever unified by a qualifying sense of personal wholeness or even personal presence. London does not live in him so much as he lives in London. That experience is plural, special, and largely taken up with naming. Wordsworth in London is an outsider, describing neither how nor what he felt but attempting, instead, to characterize the place. "That motley imagery," in his words, turns out to be just that.

Now homeward through the thickening hubbub, where
See, among the less distinguishable shapes,
The Italian, with his frame of Images

> Upon his head; with Basket at his waist
> The Jew; the stately and slow-moving Turk
> With freight of slippers piled beneath his arm.
> Briefly, we find, if tired random sights
> And haply to that search our thoughts should turn,
> Among the crowd, conspicuous less or more,
> As we proceed, all specimens of Man
> Through all the colours which the sun bestows,
> And every character of form and face,
> The Swede, the Russian; from the genial South,
> The Frenchman and the Spaniard; from remote
> America, the Hunter-Indian; Moors,
> Malays, Lascars, the Tartar and Chinese,
> And Negro Ladies in white muslin gowns.

Even in Cambridge, though not nearly so various as London, Wordsworth says he "roamed delighted, through the motley spectacle," "a mountain youth, a northern Villager." And one has the suspicion there, too, that his remoteness from Nature creates an odd self-alienation. Taken up with his essential self, a self which has assumed the properties of a partially remembered, partially imagined landscape, Wordsworth does not ever, while in any social setting, unless it be with another solitary, walk "in blessedness" as he does—by his own admission—when he is in a landscape. The city cannot do what, say, a mountain can, to shape "the measure and the prospect of a soul to majesty."

It is always Nature which brings Wordsworth back from despair and disappointment.

> . . . Behold me then
> Once more in Nature's presence, thus restored
> Or otherwise, and strengthened once again . . .
> To habits of devoutest sympathy.

No contemporary confessional poet comes back from despair and disappointment long enough to catch his breath, let alone to be restored. Nature is not part of his world. Perhaps because it seems too unified to reflect his inner disorder, perhaps because he has been so deeply urbanized, he can no longer imagine himself in its presence. Whatever the case, Nature teaches him nothing.

But what happens between Wordsworth and Nature beyond mutual generosity and restoration? Though he learns from Nature, it is very hard to know just what it is Wordsworth does learn. It is stated in the poem, though never proven, that love of Nature leads to love of man. In Wordsworth's case, love of Nature seems to lead naturally to love of self, and love of self naturally back to love of Nature. The peculiar lack of intensity in the treatment of the French Revolution in *The Prelude* leads me to doubt that it could stand as a sign of Wordsworth's love of man. Only in those strange encounters with the solitaries (the old veteran, the blind beggar) does one have a sense of his sympathetic capacity towards his fellow man. That Nature brings a "wiser mood" in which he could find "in man an object of delight and pure imagination, and of love" is something that is never convincingly demonstrated. We end up taking his word for it, while we are, perhaps, secretly sure that "love of man" is an attitude that grows from Wordsworth's own sense of well-being and consequent largesse of feeling. The grossest view of this mysterious imparting of knowledge is that without Nature as a source of inspiration, Wordsworth would not have written poems, *The Prelude* in particular. Often he begins with a vague sense of something, a shadowy recollection, and then feels his energies pick up; one begins to suspect that he writes as a way of filling out such calls to imagination. One also senses that as he writes, Nature increases in power and presence, that, in fact, the fullest embodiment of Nature is the fullest embodiment of the poet's mission, the poem. It is hard to know how true or how false this assessment is. Wordsworth does not tell us.

> Ye motions of delight, that through the fields
> Stir gently, breezes and soft airs that breathe
> The breath of Paradise, and find your way
> To the recesses of the soul! Ye brooks
> Muttering along the stones, a busy noise
> By day, a quiet one in silent night,
> And you, ye Groves, whose ministry it is
> To interpose the covert of your shades,
> Even as a sleep, betwixt the heart of man
> And the uneasy world, 'twixt man himself,
> Not seldom, and his own unquiet heart,
> Oh! that I had a music and a voice,
> Harmonious as your own, that I might tell
> What ye have done for me.

Most of the scenes and certainly the most memorable scenes in *The Prelude*—the boat-stealing scene, Mt. Snowdon, among others—take place in a spatial context which is always forcefully presented. In other words, landscape. The French philosopher Gaston Bachelard said, "Memories are motionless, and the more securely they are fixed in space, the sounder they are." Wordsworth's memories are sound, and the soundest seems to be "spots of time," sanctuaries from the flux of events. They exist as reminders of the mind's power to lift us from triviality. As long as we remember forcefully enough, the present is not able to eradicate us. And we are saved. Even if what is recalled is dreary, the imagination will imbue it with a radiance and permanence that will make it a pleasure. When Wordsworth's father dies, Wordsworth describes the bleak memory of what surrounds the event:

> All these were spectacles and sounds to which
> I often would repair and thence would drink,
> As at a fountain. . . .

He is nourished by his recollection and keeps faith in the ultimate justice of Nature. If Wordsworth's vision allowed for evil in himself, we might see his pleasure in recollecting such a scene as a way of celebrating his own survival. But he doesn't, nor does he allow for it in Nature. If Nature threatens, it does so in order to instruct, never to punish; those "severer interventions," those "huge and mighty forms that do not live like living men," are modal and exist only to lead to an encompassing and restorative good.

What is significant in Wordsworth's recollections and in his choice of surrounds is that they are landscapes, places where Nature is visible. But what is a landscape? For most people, it is a kind of painting in which a countryside is represented. That much will be recognized, though what is being looked at in particular may not be. The reality of landscape has little to do with accuracy of depiction or representation, either in the broadest or most limited sense. Nor does seeing a landscape, as Ruskin suggested one might, in terms of clearly classified schools—Heroic, Classical, Pastoral— correspond to one's experience of them. And it is probably true that no one is baffled by a landscape except when the intrusion of particulars overwhelms a clear reading of depth, or when the picture plane becomes so crowded there is no possibility of establishing the illusion of outdoor space. What is usually experienced is something general and atmospheric, an impulse to identify with a certain light or the look of a terrain. Landscape incorporates and suggests, and its horizons are never final. It represents an escape from particularity of the sort associated with limited settings, cities, say, or interiors. In a still life, for example, a person knows the number and names of the fruit and might identify other objects easily, and somehow, would be moved to. But in a landscape he would be moved to do no such thing. The experience of landscape is in many ways the experience of *The Prelude*—resonant, evident, large. One may recognize a place by the disposition of a hill or a clump of trees, as we often do in the paintings of Constable, but these are spatial designations in the broad sense. Particulars in such cases may be altered to suit the painter's whim. The painter may feel free to lengthen or shorten the branch of a tree, but he will be much more cautious and constrained to a certain precision with regard to a man's arm or a chair's leg.

It is possible that one's view of the freedom afforded the painter by Nature is a sure sign of how little he knows of the natural world, of how he does not know and cannot recognize particular trees or flowers and so assumes the generality of their representation in paintings. Such ignorance is perhaps necessary. For it is just such relief from naming and knowing that one seeks in landscape. It may be that landscape is not merely a way out of the confines of the city and the deplorable conditions which flourished along with progress, but a way out of the exhausted and claustrophobic limitations of the self; and not necessarily a self without mystery or purpose, but one so pampered, so examined, so named and renamed, that it must go elsewhere to reconstitute its energies. Landscape is a way of finding another self, larger, more general, and, possibly, more basic. It certainly was for Wordsworth, who leaves the city as if it were a prison, and who immediately experiences a new freedom and the potential for self-realization. Those "trances of thought and mountings of the mind" were destined to find the measure for the man.

To illustrate the extent to which the pure world of landscape is not a social world, I shall quote from what is claimed to be part of an English sportsman's diary. Virgil Aldrich used it as epigraph to his essay "Beauty as Feeling," in Suzanne Langer's book *Reflections on Art*.

Stranger, when you appeared there on the horizon
miles to the east, a speck silhouetted against the dawn,

you stepped on my toes and bumped into me. Did you not feel the impact?

Before you appeared this whole expanse was my body, and the light and the colors in it my mind. Then the collision occurred. Now look at me. My body is shrunken to a midget-trunk with four midget-limbs. And my mind is in a skull.

I felt the impact, Stranger. I bid you good-morning—and heartily farewell!

This is the sort of appropriation possible in landscape. The self is extended, the body is the world. It is a spell that can be broken only by the intrusion of others.

Wordsworth, at times, is not very different from the English sportsman. For he exists in landscape and figures himself as landscape. And it is this double existence which contributes to making the poet's self in *The Prelude* absolute.

> . . . Oh! then the calm
> And dead still water lay upon my mind
> Even with a weight of pleasure, and the sky
> Never before so beautiful, sank down
> Into my heart, and held me like a dream.

Here the poet *is* the Nature that holds him and Nature is what he feels. In fact, he feels so strongly that everything which is not feeling seems unreal. Inundated by vastness, not by particulars, Wordsworth is borne into Nature.

> Thus daily were my sympathies enlarged,
> And thus the common range of visible things
> Grew dear to me. . . .

His vision grew with his sympathies. And when he was older his sympathies grew in an effort to overcome loss that comes with age. The vividness of Wordsworth's landscape was born out of urgency. It is the experience of loss that permits the artist to recompose. He builds from "least suggestions," "vanishings," ghosts of events. He puts together what he knows dimly and sheds his own light on it and makes it better known. The self is necessarily involved in this knowing, for in this way it reveals itself—reveals itself as the world it would have revitalized.

Views of the Mysterious Hill: The Appearance of Parnassus in American Poetry

I intend to take a close look at four American poems in which hills appear, and try to show that the hills are actually the same hill. This may seem either absurd or willful, but the hill I have in mind is the hill dearest to poetry, the hill that used to be a mountain before poetry was relegated to the marginal place it now holds. It is, of course, Parnassus, the mythological home of Apollo and the muses, and, more recently, the figurative resting place of the great poets.

It is unlikely that any of us, upon finding a hill in a poem, would think immediately of Parnassus. The chances are that some generic rise, a slope or lump lifting from a horizontal, would come to mind. Its particularity would depend on the poem's power to urge specific properties upon our vision. In the poems I shall examine, specific properties are at a minimum.

A few months ago, I was rereading some of Edwin Arlington Robinson's poems, among them "The House on the Hill," a poem I had always liked, but, as it turned out, had never read with any care, believing it was little more than an exercise, a pleasant evocation of loss and nostalgia.

The House on the Hill

They are all gone away,
 The House is shut and still,
There is nothing more to say.

Through broken walls and gray
 The winds blow bleak and shrill:
They are all gone away.

Nor is there one to-day
 To speak them good or ill:
There is nothing more to say.

Why is it then we stray
 Around the sunken sill?
They are all gone away.

And our poor fancy-play
 For them is wasted skill:
There is nothing more to say.

There is ruin and decay
 In the House on the Hill:
They are all gone away,
There is nothing more to say.

This is a dark poem that invites no rejoinder. The people are gone, and there is nothing more to say, or so it would appear, until we are told "nor is there one to-day / To speak them good or ill." At that point, we must wonder just who the departed were, and wonder why we would pass judgment on them if they were ordinary inhabitants of an ordinary house. The statement hints at something more than just our incapacity to gossip about the dead. It suggests our incapacity to judge our forebears. And who were our forebears? Why do we stray around the sunken sill? Something unnatural is happening. It is as if the house had a mysterious property that held our attention, compelled our interest beyond what might be considered a normal time span. And who are the "we" that are so drawn, so morbidly drawn, to ruin and decay, and what is their relation to the poet?

What could their "poor fancy-play" be but the practice of poetry, the play of fancy. Their skill is wasted because those for whom it is practiced are gone. But the poem could also be a judgment leveled by the past upon the present—which would make the last stanza more severe than it already appears. That is, the ruin and decay in the house on the hill might also belong to the "we," might be the outcome of their play in the absence of anyone to appreciate it. The whole poem might simply be a projection of their inability to imagine anything comparable to what their poetic forebears imagined. It would not be the first time Americans felt inadequate in front of a ruin or reminder of something that flourished at an earlier time. Nor would it be the first time a poet belittled his efforts in relation to the work of his predecessors, and shruggingly admitted, as Robinson does, "There is nothing more to say."

The poem may begin as a lament for the departed owners of the house, but it ends as a statement of grief for the poet and his colleagues' own failed powers of speech. If, as I have been implying, the hill is Parnassus (and if the house of poetry is empty), would not that leave us, or whoever the "we" are, with nothing to say? Are not the muses and the great poets the source and foundation of all our inspired utterance? The plain repetitions of Robinson's poem would serve as proof of our impoverishment if they didn't work so well as refrains within an elaborate system of retrievals. Robinson's choice of the villanelle was ideal for his subject. Of all forms, the villanelle does most to suggest recovery; its repeated lines, the circularity of its stanzas, seem a repudiation of forward motion, of temporality, and, finally, of dissolution. This may be why it is the form of some of our period's most celebrated poems of loss. I am thinking specifically of Dylan Thomas's "Do not go gentle into that good night" and Elizabeth Bishop's "One Art," which, as it happens, is the art of losing.

In Robinson's poem, this counter-motion suggests that even if the muses, Apollo, the old masters are all gone away—making it appear that without their sustaining example there is nothing more to say—all is not lost. American poets have a tendency to clear the decks of whatever preceded them, so that they can begin again, have the illusion at least that they are starting from scratch. They tend not to build on the past so much as wipe it away. Their need to claim originality has produced a remarkably consistent set of topoi, or places that are simultaneously real and metaphorical, where their Americanness is unmistakable. The seashore, say, is one that begins with Whitman and Longfellow and continues through to Bishop and Lowell. Wallace Stevens's bare, winter landscape is another. An abandoned hill may be yet another.

Poem 399 in Emily Dickinson's *Collected Poems* bears some resemblance to the Robinson poem.

> A House upon the Height—
> That Wagon never reached—
> No Dead, were ever carried down—
> No Peddler's Cart—approached—
>
> Whose Chimney never smoked—
> Whose Windows—Night and Morn—
> Caught Sunrise first—and Sunset—last—
> Then—held an Empty Pane—
>
> Whose fate—Conjecture knew—
> No other neighbor—did—
> And what it was—we never lisped—
> Because He—never told—

The house in Emily Dickinson's poem is not a ruin. It has windows and a chimney. But between sunset and sunrise no one can be seen to move behind its windows, and its chimney never smokes. It would seem not to be inhabited by creatures like ourselves. In fact, its distance from our world is what is stressed. It occupies a place apart, a rather privileged place, since the one connection it has to us is the absolute one of witnessing the beginning and the end of days—catching sunrise first and sunset last. The height on which it sits appears to be more than any mere hill, and the mysterious invisibility of its inhabitant suggests that it is a heavenly mansion. But why should it have such earthly features as chimney and windows, and why should its isolation be measured by its never having been reached by wagons or peddlers' carts, unless a compromise were being sought regarding its heavenly status?

In the first line of the last stanza, we are told that only Conjecture knew the fate of the house. Conjecture is personified, and thus becomes the odd antecedent of He in the poem's last line, a silent He, or at least one who does not tell us what he knows. If he did tell us, he would cease to exist, and in his place we would have Fact or Certainty or some other figure for whom speculation and invention were wholly unnecessary. In other words, to know the fate of this particular house would obviate the need or the call to imagine. The god who keeps track of the sun is Apollo, the god of poetry. To wonder about the fate of Apollo's house is to consider the fate of poetry. This poem betrays some anxiety about the fate of poetry, especially the fate of its author's poetry. Conjecture, or Imagination, does not reveal the future because it can't, but because its particular truths are not validated or invalidated by what will come to pass. And even if Conjecture were to reveal this secret fate, "we"—we poets and concerned neighbors—could only repeat it imperfectly, lisping. Dickinson's anxiety is not unusual for an American poet. Parnassus is not your ordinary hill, and being so far away it is not a place—though mythical—that can be taken for granted. For who knows if what worked in the past and on another continent will work again, and in a new place?

We look to Stevens's poem "Mrs. Alfred Uruguay."

So what said the others and the sun went down
And, in the brown blues of evening, the lady said,
In the donkey's ear, "I fear that elegance
Must struggle like the rest." She climbed until
The moonlight in her lap, mewing her velvet,
And her dress were one and she said, "I have said no
To everything, in order to get at myself.
I have wiped away moonlight like mud. Your innocent ear
And I, if I rode naked, are what remain."

The moonlight crumbled to degenerate forms,
While she approached the real, upon her mountain,
With lofty darkness. The donkey was there to ride,
To hold by the ear, even though it wished for a bell,
Wished faithfully for a falsifying bell.
Neither the moonlight could change it. And for her,
To be, regardless of velvet, could never be more
Than to be, she could never differently be,
Her no and no made yes impossible.

Who was it passed her there on a horse all will,
What figure of capable imagination?
Whose horse clattered on the road on which she rose,
As it descended, blind to her velvet and
The moonlight? Was it a rider intent on the sun,
A youth, a lover with phosphorescent hair,
Dressed poorly, arrogant of his streaming forces,
Lost in an integration of the martyrs' bones,
Rushing from what was real; and capable?

The villages slept as the capable man went down,
Time swished on the village clocks and dreams were alive,
The enormous gongs gave edges to their sounds,
As the rider, no chevalere and poorly dressed,
Impatient of the bells and midnight forms,
Rode over the picket rocks, rode down the road,
And, capable, created in his mind,
Eventual victor, out of the martyrs' bones,
The ultimate elegance: the imagined land.

What do we see in those "brown blues of evening"? All we
can be sure of is that a well-dressed woman is riding a donkey up a mountain and a poorly dressed youth is riding a
horse down the same mountain. But the height of the mountain, and what grass grew beside the road, the disposition of
the villages that lay, presumably, at the foot of the mountain,
are shadowy at best. What matters is that the ascent of someone named Mrs. Alfred Uruguay coincides with a personal
quest that bears some resemblance to writing. To conquer
Parnassus, she must get at herself, get to the bottom of who

she is. One might say that all poets earn their place on Parnassus by getting to the bottom of the page, entertaining the happy illusion that when they finish what they are working on, they will be farther along their chosen route than when they began. It is a sustaining vision of purpose that many poets share, although not often publicly, because it seems too grandiose an aim, and of course it is constantly being undermined by the humdrum character of reality.

Anyway, Mrs. Alfred Uruguay is riding a donkey up a mountain, whispering in the donkey's ear, admitting that in order to get at herself she has had to say "no to everything." This sounds preposterous coming from a woman garbed in velvet, who wipes away the prettifying moonlight as if it were mud, and accepts the fact that she, in her elegance, must struggle like the rest. The severity of her commitment has been likened to Stevens's own propensity for reduction, which, at its most extreme, calls for "a mind of winter." Mrs. Alfred Uruguay's drive towards greater simplicity represents a strong puritanical strain in her character, and locates her impulse to reimagine herself along plainer lines as recognizably American.

Her noble intentions, however, are of no consequence to her audience, the donkey, whose appetite for reality does not exceed its need for illusion. "It wished for a bell, / Wished faithfully for a falsifying bell." How like the reading public, one might venture, the one that complains of the sadness and seriousness of poetry and wonders disingenuously why poems can't be happier or at least simpler and more straightforward. Any "no and no" that made "yes" impossible was not something the donkey—or any donkey—wished to hear. The peculiarity of a woman wearing velvet and whispering to a donkey what she must do makes the scene both comic and hopeless. But what makes it strangely believable is that her journey should be uphill. Difficulty has a way of validating most ventures. And Mrs. Alfred Uruguay's hill? Is it, as some have suggested, Montevideo (or Mount of Vision), the capital city of Uruguay? There is no doubt that a vision of her essential self is what Mrs. Uruguay seeks. But does a woman ever find her true self in her husband's name? Surely not, and surely not one with a calling as severe as Mrs. Uruguay's.

When the poorly dressed youth, the figure of capable imagination on the way down the mountain, passes her, the poem suddenly changes. Mrs. Uruguay's calling, it becomes clear, is not to undertake bizarre measures in a course of self-improvement but to write poetry. As if to deepen the nocturnal drama of the poem, Stevens asks three leading questions whose intent is to reveal the identity of the youth. They are heavy with attribution, so heavy that the rider's blindness to Mrs. Uruguay, her moonlight and velvet, is oddly, uncomfortably conflated with what must be the horse's response as well. Still, the questions make it clear that the youth and Mrs. Uruguay are opposites. He rides a horse, she a donkey; he is a figure of capable imagination, she a figure of little or no imagination ("for her, / To be . . . could never be more / Than to be"); he is lost in an integration (or reverie) of the martyrs' bones, she is the unfolding tale of her own martyrdom; he is rushing from what was real, she is slowly approaching the real; he is Apollo exercising his privilege and leaving the precincts of Parnassus, she is the struggling poet, climbing Parnassus in hopes her effort will be rewarded with a "yes" that outlasts the economies of being.

The questions playfully circle the identity of the youth. To be intent on the sun is what we might expect of the sun god, but to give him phosphorescent hair is almost to overstate the case. And to make him "arrogant of his streaming forces," which is to say, I suppose, proud of his radiant energies, is practically to answer the question of his identity. He travels down through the sleeping villages, impatient with all that surrounds him, as he creates in his mind the ultimate elegance—the imagined land. He leaves Parnassus to the likes of Mrs. Alfred Uruguay, perhaps because it is an irrelevant reality, not needed if the martyrs' bones (the literary remains of the great poets) are the portable stuff from which the ultimate elegance can be made. And it may be too exclusive a domain: the new Parnassus, if there is to be one, must be democratic, and there must be enough of it to go around. The youth is poorly dressed as a sign that wealth, or any sign of privilege—even the privilege of mythology— is unnecessary. He appears as a distinctly American incarnation of Apollo. Apollo as a visionary cowboy.

For Mrs. Alfred Uruguay, however, Parnassus is the old Parnassus, existing as a monolithic entity, a place of obdurate privilege, a mecca to which every poetry aspirant must make a pilgrimage. She is dressed for the occasion but has picked an especially slow and inappropriate means of ascent. It would have been more in keeping with her privilege to have been carried to the giddy heights by inspiration alone, or at the very least by a winged horse—in any case, to have been airborne. If there is a point to this poem, with its peculiar crossing of impulses, it is that the true occasions for and places of poetry are internal. Anything else is a cheat, as we can be reasonably sure Mrs. Alfred Uruguay will discover. Like the hill-poems of Robinson and Dickinson, this poem may be a case of the anxiety produced in the American poet by the traditional view of Parnassus. It hints at the possibility that we, having arrived so late on the scene of poetry, may be left out, that there may be no room for us on the old Parnassus, and that our only immortality lies in the imagined land, that place we have created out of the martyrs' bones—the place where we shall leave our own bones.

Now I'd like to look at a poem by Anthony Hecht.

A Hill

In Italy, where this sort of thing can occur,
I had a vision once—though you understand
It was nothing at all like Dante's, or the visions of saints,
And perhaps not a vision at all. I was with some friends,
Picking my way through a warm sunlit piazza
In the early morning. A clear fretwork of shadows
From huge umbrellas littered the pavement and made
A sort of lucent shallows in which was moored
A small navy of carts. Books, coins, old maps,
Cheap landscapes and ugly religious prints
Were all on sale. The colors and noise
Like the flying hands were gestures of exultation,
So that even the bargaining

Rose to the ear like a voluble godliness.
And then, when it happened, the noises suddenly stopped,
And it got darker; pushcarts and people dissolved
And even the great Farnese Palace itself
Was gone, for all its marble; in its place
Was a hill, mole-colored and bare. It was very cold,
Close to freezing, with a promise of snow.
The trees were like old ironwork gathered for scrap
Outside a factory wall. There was no wind,
And the only sound for a while was the little click
Of ice as it broke in the mud under my feet.
I saw a piece of ribbon snagged on a hedge,
But no other sign of life. And then I heard
What seemed the crack of a rifle. A hunter, I guessed;
At least I was not alone. But just after that
Came the soft and papery crash
Of a great branch somewhere unseen falling to earth.

And that was all, except for the cold and silence
That promised to last forever, like the hill.

Then prices came through, and fingers, and I was restored
To the sunlight and my friends. But for more than a week
I was scared by the plain bitterness of what I had seen.
All this happened about ten years ago,
And it hasn't troubled me since, but at last, today,
I remembered that hill; it lies just to the left
Of the road north of Poughkeepsie; and as a boy
I stood before it for hours in wintertime.

After announcing he had a vision once, and sensing the grandiosity of his claim, the poet in a series of rapid disclaimers says that his vision was nothing like Dante's or the visions of saints, and might not be a vision at all. Thus, at the outset, in a gesture that is half-modest and half-defensive, he shies from any comparison with the illustrious dead. The vision that might not have been a vision occurs while the narrator is picking his way among things for sale in a warm sunlit piazza. It is winter; the only signs of life are a ribbon snagged on a hedge and a sound like the crack of a rifle, suggesting that there is a hunter in the vicinity. Then, in lines reminiscent of Frost's "The Most of It," the narrator describes the crash of a great branch somewhere unseen falling to earth, and says, "that was all except for the cold and silence / That promised to last forever. . . ." He recalls, ten years later, that for more than a week he was scared by the bitterness of what he had seen. The hill is revealed, at poem's end, to be north of Poughkeepsie.

A poem as straightforward as this one should not present a problem, but it does. The problem is what to make of the hill. Why it should appear, and why, having appeared, it should frighten the narrator, and why it should take him ten years finally to place it are all vexing questions. But most vexing is: Why would a boy stand before it for hours in wintertime? Would anyone stand before it for long and not freeze or be driven indoors? The hill must have had some pull on the boy, something that he felt then, but was reluctant to acknowledge as an adult until it came back to him in Italy like a lost piece of his American past. At this point, I would like to say that the hill, like all the other hills I have

discussed, was Parnassus, that it was a vision, a sudden revelation of the estranged narrator's real roots, that as a boy he
considered not the hill but his own fate or destiny, which
was, though he may not have known it then, to be a poet,
that the hill would come back to haunt him, to remind him
of an essential loneliness that is American, as American as
Robert Frost. I would like to, but I can't.

Part of the poem's beauty is that it resists, in its careful and
cadenced disclosures, any reduction, any reading, in fact, of
the hill. And the hill's resolute plainness seems a rebuke to
making of it anything more than it is. Despite the wintry
eeriness in which it appears (something like that of the
dream landscape in the film *Spellbound*), and despite its
power to mesmerize a boy for hours in wintertime, it is just a
hill near Poughkeepsie. It resists interpretation. But perhaps
it resists too much; perhaps in its plainness it is Parnassus
after all, Parnassus wearing its American disguise as a plain
hill. Maybe for American poets Parnassus—especially when
it appears in a place that gave birth to the visions of Dante
and the saints—must appear in the cold air of winter and be
mole-colored and bare. And maybe this is the most perfect
example of how it haunts us, how it will appear unexpect-
edly—as just a hill we once saw—and appear again, and
again.

The President's Resignation

Early this evening, the President announced his resignation. Though his rise to power was meteoric, he was not a popular leader. He made no promises before taking office but speculated endlessly about the kind of weather we would have during his term, sometimes even making a modest prediction. And when, as it happened from time to time, his prediction was not borne out, he would quickly conceal his disappointment. His critics accused him of spending too much energy on such exercises, and were especially severe about his wasting public funds on a National Museum of Weather, in whose rooms one could experience the climate of any day anywhere in the history of man. His war on fluorocarbons, known as the "gas crusade," is still talked about with astonishment. Among those attending the President's farewell address were: the First Minister of Potential Clearness & husband, the Warden of Inner and Outer Darkness & husband, the Deputy Chief of Lesser Degrees & wife, the First Examiner of Ambiguous Customs & two secretaries, the Chief of Transcendent Decorum & friend, the Assistant Magistrate of Exemplary Conditions & two friends, the Undersecretary for Devices Appropriate to Conditions Unspecific & mother, the Lord Chancellor of Abnormal

Silences & father, the Deputy Examiner of Fallibility and Remorse & daughters, the Chief Poet Laureate and Keeper of Glosses for Unwritten Texts & follower.

THE PRESIDENT'S FAREWELL ADDRESS

Ladies and gentlemen, friends and colleagues, thank you for coming this evening. I know how difficult for you the past few days have been and how sad you must be tonight. But I came to the Presidency from the bottom of my heart and leave it with the best will in the world. And I believe I have weathered my term without betraying the trust of the people. From the beginning I have preached melancholy and invention, nostalgia and prophecy. The languors of art have been my haven. More than anything I wished to be the first truly modern President, and to make my term the free extension of impulse and the preservation of chance.

(Applause)

Who can forget my proposals, petitions uttered on behalf of those who labored in the great cause of weather—measuring wind, predicting rain, giving themselves to whole generations of days—whose attention was ever riveted to the invisible wheel that turns the stars and to the stars themselves? How like poetry, said my enemies. They were right. For it was my wish to make nothing happen. Thank heaven it has been so, for my words would easily have been wasted along with the works they might have engendered. I have always spoken for what does not change, for what resists action, for the stillness at the center of man.

(Applause)

Thus we have been privileged to celebrate fifty-one national holidays, the fifty-one days I hesitated before taking office — the glorious fifty-one that now belong to the annals of meditation. How lovely the mind is when overcast or clouded with indecision, when it goes nowhere, when it is conscious, radiantly conscious, of its own secret motions.

(Applause)

And the hours spent reading Chekhov aloud to you, my beloved Cabinet! The delirium of our own unimportance that followed! How we sighed and moaned for the frailty of our lives! Not to be remembered in two hundred years, or even in two! And the silence that was ours, each of us overtaken with a feeling of moments prolonged, magically chronicled in the stillness of windows beyond which the minute changes of the world went on.

(Applause)

Friends, how can I tell you what weather has meant! The blue sky, its variations and repetitions, is what I look back on: the blues of my first day in office, the blues of my fifth day, the porcelain blues, the monotonous blues, the stately blues, the ideal blues, and the slightly less than ideal blues, the yellow blues on certain winter days. Always the great cupola of light, a vague yet luminous crown, spread with tireless regularity, turning the prose of my life into exultation and desire. And then it would dim into twilight and the green edge of the world would darken. Finally the weather of night would arrive, under which I drifted as if my bed were a ship—the monstrous openness of night, in which birds become lost, in which sounds travel with a melancholy beyond tears, in which my dreams of a golden age seem, for a moment, diminished and hopelessly exiled. I have sailed and sailed my whole life.

(Applause)

I remember each morning, when I was young, setting out to cross the plains of boredom, over which small islands of shadow drifted according to the caprice of clouds. Little did I know that those days had historical importance. Airy monuments, blurred remembrances were being built, suggested, removed almost in the instant of their occurrence. Each morning, crossing those plains, armed only with desire for sympathy and adulation, I was even then forming the role I would play as President. The emptiness of those days was as deep and relentless as the breathing of parents. When would the world awake and acknowledge its light, that airy gold in which strange domes of gray paraded soundlessly, far off?

(Applause)

I have never ceased looking up at the sky and I never shall. The azures and ultramarines of disappointment and joy come only from it. The blessings of weather shall always exceed the office of our calling and turn our words, without warning, into the petals of a huge and inexhaustible rose. Thank you and good-bye.

ACKNOWLEDGMENTS

Thanks to the editors of the following publications in which some of these writings first appeared:

THE BEST AMERICAN POETRY 1991 (Scribner): Introduction to *The Best American Poetry 1991*

COLUMBIA REVIEW: "Introduction to Joseph Brodsky"

THE CONTINUOUS LIFE (Alfred A. Knopf, 1990): "Translation," "Narrative Poetry"

GETTYSBURG REVIEW: "Views of the Mysterious Hill: The Appearance of Parnassus in American Poetry"

GRAND STREET: "Fantasia on the Relations Between Poetry and Photography"

LITERARY IMAGINATION: "A Poet's Alphabet"

THE NEW YORKER: "Poetic Justice," "The President's Resignation"

POETS AND CRITICS READ VERGIL, edited by Sarah Spence (Yale University Press, 1999): "Some Observations of *Aeneid* Book VI"

POETS ON POETRY: "Notes on the Craft of Poetry"

PROSE: "Landscape and the Poetry of Self"

A NOTE ABOUT THE AUTHOR

Mark Strand was born in Summerside, Prince Edward Island, Canada, and was raised and educated in the United States. He has written nine books of poems, which have brought him many honors and grants, including a MacArthur Fellowship and the 1999 Pulitzer Prize for his book of poems *Blizzard of One*. He was chosen as Poet Laureate of the United States in 1990. He is the author of a book of stories, *Mr. and Mrs. Baby*, several volumes of translations (of works by Rafael Alberti and Carlos Drummond de Andrade, among others), the editor of a number of anthologies, and author of two monographs on contemporary artists (William Bailey and Edward Hopper). He teaches in the Committee on Social Thought at the University of Chicago.

A NOTE ON THE TYPE

The text of this book was set in Electra, a typeface designed by W. A. Dwiggins (1880–1956). This face cannot be classified as either modern or old style. It is not based on any historical model, nor does it echo any particular period or style. It avoids the extreme contrasts between thick and thin elements that mark most modern faces, and it attempts to give a feeling of fluidity, power, and speed.

Composed by NK Graphics, Keene, New Hampshire
Printed and bound by R. R. Donnelley and Sons,
Harrisonburg, Virginia
Designed by Virginia Tan